Palgrave Studies in Family Business Heterogeneity

Contemporary family business research has been moving from highlighting the differences between family and non-family firms to the differences among family firms owing to the financial and non-financial dynamics that influences the strategic decisions and family firm actions. While a prominent stream of research draws attention to financial and non-financial goals (such as socioemotional wealth preservation) and other factors, we still do not know enough about such idiosyncrasies. This series will take a closer look at both financial and non-financial family firm idiosyncrasies across the globe and consider the ecosystem (i.e., regulatory framework, values, culture, access to finance, markets, R&D, and technology), and other national and economic conditions that allow the operations and presence of family firms.

Roland E. Kidwell

Dysfunction and Deviance Across Family Firms

Varying Reflections of the Dark Side

palgrave
macmillan

Roland E. Kidwell
Florida Atlantic University
Boca Raton, FL, USA

ISSN 2662-6055 ISSN 2662-6063 (electronic)
Palgrave Studies in Family Business Heterogeneity
ISBN 978-3-031-51815-7 ISBN 978-3-031-51816-4 (eBook)
https://doi.org/10.1007/978-3-031-51816-4

This Palgrave Macmillan imprint is published by the registered company Springer Nature Switzerland AG
The registered company address is: Gewerbestrasse 11, 6330 Cham, Switzerland

Paper in this product is recyclable.

This work is dedicated to Linda Achey Kidwell, Ph.D., my lifetime partner in everything.

Series Editors' Preface

The ongoing interactions between a family and a business can result in multiple outcomes that range from the most positive ones to the less desirable ones. Over the latter, researchers in the family business field have argued that the future of a firm is at stake when its stakeholders misbehave. Furthermore, deviance and misfortune represent elements that mainstream media have used by aggravating these problems that may result in destructive consequences. As a result, there is a need to properly understand better how these forces matter and what can be done to minimize their negative outcomes.

As deviance and dysfunctional behaviors represent topics of interest and importance that deserve attention, we extended an invitation to Dr. Roland Kidwell, a world-renowned research expert in the field, to author this book titled "*Dysfunction and Deviance Across Family Firms.*" Now, it is our distinct pleasure and honor to present this new addition to the *Palgrave Studies in Family Business Heterogeneity*.

The book focuses on the growing body of research across families, firms, levels of analysis, and types of behaviors, and offers insights into some important issues relevant to cross-disciplinary research and how these might be addressed in detail with further inquiry. Throughout the book, Dr. Kidwell organized the several causes of deviance and dysfunctions, and how these behaviors not only affect the internal organization of the family firm, but also spill over to the external environment. He later offered interesting connections of particular constructs that transcends the family system and concludes with future research directions.

It is indeed vitally important to understand if family firms are resilient enough to survive after the dysfunctional behavior of particular family and/or non-family stakeholders. Especially, family firms have daily duties to remain competitive in the market and strive to offer value to all their stakeholders. Coping with dysfunctional behaviors represents another layer that can set examples to learn or even follow.

Often times, some of the aspiring entrepreneurs avoid the inclusion of family members into their nascent venture projects in order to prevent future conflicts. However, deviant behavior does not occur in all family firms, and it can be prevented or minimized. Therefore, we believe that this book can be helpful for understanding better the causes and antecedents of deviance and dysfunctional behaviors, and how these issues can be addressed effectively.

We expect family business scholars and practitioners in general to find this book highly useful and enlightening about this important topic.

Greensboro, USA — Esra Memili
Jonesboro, USA — Erick P. C. Chang

Acknowledgments

The author wishes to thank the many scholars who have contributed over the years to the important research topic of negative behaviors in family firms, in families, and elsewhere in organizations. Whereas deviance and dysfunction are crucial areas for past, present, and future research, these bad behaviors should not overshadow the hard work done by family firm leaders, family business consultants, educators, and others who attempt to address the antecedents of potentially dysfunctional behavior before it infects the workplace. These efforts seem to be successful based on the results of the day-to-day struggle involved in operating a successful family business and the long-term efforts of engaging future generations as stewards to keep that business moving forward. In the newspaper industry—where I was first employed as a reporter and then an editor—it used to be said that when dog bites man it's not news, but when man bites dog it's news. Thus, dysfunctional behavior among families and family businesses, due to its relative rarity, is news that grabs the attention of the media, the producers of television shows and movies (some good, some bad), or the folks who just enjoy hearing about others' misfortune. I appreciate and thank those family firm leaders and members who have confidentially shared their stories—good and bad—with me. Some of these stories are included in this book.

After several years of research on dysfunction and deviance in family firms and related topics, I thank the many researchers I have had the pleasure of collaborating with over the years, specifically the scholars who worked with me in undertaking a recent review of the literature in family firm dysfunction, which informs some of the content of this book: Linda Kidwell, Kimberly Eddleston, Jim Cater, and Ellison Howard. I also wish to thank Hasselt University's Research Center for Entrepreneurship and Family Firms, which hosted me in Belgium where I completed the book while on sabbatical from Florida Atlantic University. Special thanks to Drs. Wim Voordeckers and Anneleen Michiels at UHasselt for their gracious invitation, assistance, and hospitality during my visit. I also wish to thank the Fulbright US Scholar program and the Fulbright Commission of Belgium for providing financial help and other support during my stay. Thanks also to Drs. Esra Memili and Clay Dibrell for asking me to write a chapter for their book on heterogeneity in family firms, and Drs. Memili and Erick Chang for following that up with the idea to take it one step further by expanding that chapter into a book. Finally, thanks go out to my family—Linda, Kelly, Tracy, and Rosalind—for always keeping me on my toes, love you all.

Contents

List of Tables

CHAPTER 1

Dysfunctional Families, Dysfunctional Firms?

Abstract How dysfunctional and deviant behaviors develop, occur, and are viewed within and across family firms is vastly different than similar behaviors in other types of businesses due to characteristics that are unique to family firms as well as the differences across family firms and the environments in which they operate. Characteristics that are expected to indicated differences in the presence of deviance and dysfunction include long-standing interactions starting in childhood among individuals, the family system, and the firm; how the family pursues its non-economic as well as its economic goals, and the nature of the dominant family's values and the degree to which they are adopted by the firm. This chapter defines major terms, poses key questions that will be addressed, and lays out plans for the rest of the book.

Keywords Dysfunctional behavior · Deviant behavior · Family business · Heterogeneity · Family values · Trust · Oversight

> *Trusted bookkeeper swindled €92,000 from a family business by selling construction materials at discount prices*

R. E. Kidwell, *Dysfunction and Deviance Across Family Firms*, Palgrave Studies in Family Business Heterogeneity,
https://doi.org/10.1007/978-3-031-51816-4_1

How a family firm that sold a pipe dream for holidaymakers spiraled out of control
A Gucci family secret: Heiress alleges she was sexually abused from age 6 onward
At Siemens, Bribery was Just a Line Item

This collection of recent headlines reveals a small part of the story of dysfunctional and deviant behavior at family firms—large and small, well-known and unknown. Yet, the topics of dysfunction and deviance have been the focus of researchers in the social sciences for more than 100 years. This research dates at least as far back as Ringelmann's rope-pulling experiments in which productivity losses were tied to participants' lowering their efforts to hide in the crowd, a behavior later termed social loafing (Latané et al., 1979). Fast forwarding to the twenty-first century, the study of all manner of dysfunctional behavior in family firms has become a hot topic for academic research as well as fodder for a hungry media. On the academic side, this is particularly relevant considering that differences are being discovered in the causes and effects of the behaviors that are studied, that some family firms and family firm employees are more prone to dysfunction and deviance than others, and that the negative impact of these behaviors is felt not only within the family firm but in the surrounding environment. On the media side, public feuds among families and business failures just make for good stories.

Only a few dysfunctional acts result in headlines but nonetheless have deleterious effects. Case studies into dysfunction and deviance in family firms indicate that various types of bad behaviors occur, and they may develop and be handled differently depending on the firm and the players involved. For example, a family member of a small business in Florida was found to have stolen more than $50,000 from the family firm over several years. She not only kept her job when the theft was discovered, but her CEO uncle gave her a raise because he believed she was underpaid and in some way entitled to the money she stole. In another situation, at an Irish family firm, the trusted bookkeeper in the first headline above stole more than €92,000 by selling the company's construction materials at a discount, keeping the money, and falsifying company accounts to hide his illegal actions. When the family discovered the theft and confronted the non-family employee, he apologized and explained that he took the money to help pay for his daughter's medical care and described his breach of trust to the family as a lousy thing to do. The family firm fired the bookkeeper and turned him in to the authorities.

These examples illustrate that family and non-family members are often treated differently for basically committing the same offense; other instances show that in some family firms such behavior may be more likely to occur than in others. As will be seen throughout this book, research into dysfunction in the family business involves the study of a wide range of behaviors that include poor work performance, theft, fraud, discrimination against non-family employees (also known as bifurcation bias), interpersonal aggression (bullying and violence), gender discrimination, bribery, corruption, and tax evasion. Thus, family firm research has begun to focus on at least two dimensions: 1. differences in the types and causes of dysfunctional behavior that are observed and 2. differences in the degree of dysfunction from firm to firm.

The purpose of this book is to discuss this growing body of research across families, firms, levels of analysis, and types of behaviors, and offer insights into some important relationships across disciplines found in the research and how these might be addressed in detail with further inquiry. The book does not intend to review all research related to the topic of dysfunction and deviance in family firms. Rather, it intends to highlight studies related to differences across family firms in what leads to dysfunction and deviant behavior, the vast diversity in the types of negative behaviors that occur in family firms, and the differential impact these behaviors have inside and outside family businesses.

As a starting point, key terms need to be clarified. Family firm heterogeneity is defined here as "the range of categorical and/or variational difference(s) between or among family firms at a given time or across time" (Daspit et al., 2021: 298). Second, although the definition of "family" is evolving as will be seen later in the book and the difficulty in definitively defining a family business is clear (Diaz-Moriana et al., 2019), a family business is characterized in this book by its behavior and the degree to which it indicates "the intention to shape or pursue the vision of the business held by a dominant coalition controlled by members of the same family or a small number of families in a manner that is potentially sustainable across generations of the family or families" (Chua et al., 1999: 25). Yet, how are the key elements of dysfunction and deviance—potential threats to the vibrance and sustainability of the family firm—to be defined? They both seem to be seen in a negative light and represent a dark side of organizational behavior. But what are the distinctions between the two and how do they relate to family firms?

Sociologist Robert Merton first developed a theory of deviance to explain criminal behavior by focusing on the discrepancy between the achievement of wealth and the inability of many in society to obtain it (Merton, 1957). Those individuals who valued wealth but could not get it through accepted means became deviants by turning to crime. In organizations, the dark side of human behavior has taken on different names and definitions in the last 30 years of workplace research. Deviance (Mackey et al., 2021; Robinson & Bennett, 1995), dysfunction (Griffin et al., 1998), workplace misbehavior (Vardi & Weitz, 2004), anti-social behavior (Giacalone & Greenberg, 1997), and counterproductive work behavior (Spector et al., 2006; Marcus et al., 2016) are labels attached to actions that can have negative consequences for individuals, their organizations, and the external environment. In more recent years, family business researchers have focused on negative behavior in family firms, its antecedents, and its outcomes on individual and firm performance (e.g., Ding et al., 2016; Eddleston & Mulki, 2021; Kidwell et al., 2012; Madison et al., 2018; O'Brien et al., 2018; Temouri et al., 2022).

Dysfunctional and deviant behaviors are sometimes placed under the same conceptual umbrella, but there are important distinctions. Attempting to provide a more universal term for various conceptions of "bad" behavior including deviance, Griffin and Lopez (2005: 1000) defined dysfunctional behavior as "motivated behavior by an employee or group of employees that is intended to have negative consequences for another individual and/or group and/or the organization itself." Such behavior can damage individuals, their families, their organizations, and in some instances the firm's external environment. Deviant behavior in organizations has been traditionally defined in a somewhat similar vein: "(V)oluntary behavior that violates significant organizational norms and, in doing so, threatens the well-being of the organization, its members, or both" (Bennett & Robinson, 2000: 349). But as several researchers have pointed out over the years, deviance may not necessarily threaten the well-being of the organization, that would depend on the content of the norms and the behaviors that violate those norms, i.e., not all norms are positive (Locke, 2003; Mainemelis, 2010). Thus, research has focused on such concepts as constructive, positive, and even strategic deviance (e.g., Spreitzer & Sonenshein, 2004; Lin et al., 2016; Vadera et al., 2013; Aguilera et al., 2018; Kidwell & Nygaard, 2011).

In addition, the negative acts that constitute dysfunctional behavior may in some instances be beneficial to the family and the family firm but harmful to others inside and outside it. Among these negative actions are bifurcation bias, bribery, corruption, fraud, and corporate social irresponsibility. These varied outcomes illustrate the ambiguity of dysfunctional behavior as well as deviance: "The intent in breaking a norm may be constructive or destructive, the result of breaking a norm may be positive or negative, and the decision to engage in deviant behavior may be strategically positive for the organization" (Kidwell et al., 2019: 655). Similarly, the family firm may engage in what could be viewed as bad behavior (discrimination against non-family members) but is advantageous not only to the benefitting family members but also to the firm's long-term sustainability by hiring and promoting family members who are committed to the family business (Jaskiewicz et al., 2013). Likewise, a family firm may find it difficult to do business in some economic and political environments without engaging in what is apparently dysfunctional behavior such as bribing officials to gain access to local markets or other types of corruption.

How dysfunctional and deviant behaviors develop, occur, and are viewed within and across family firms is vastly different from similar behaviors in other types of businesses. Particularly, family firms possess unique characteristics and there are differences across family firms given the environments in which they operate. These features include interactions between the individual, the family system, and the firm (Tagiuri & Davis, 1992), the degree to which and the reasons why the family pursues socioemotional wealth (Gomez-Mejia et al., 2007; Swab et al., 2020), the unique organizational ecosystem in which family organizations operate (De Massis et al., 2021), and the nature of the dominant family's values and the degree to which they are adopted by the firm (Rau et al., 2019).

On the one hand, unlike non-family firms, family businesses have family members and family managers/owners whose stewardship values may lead them to serve as "an additional layer of oversight," against the occurrence of fraudulent and other dysfunctional behaviors (Astrachan et al., 2020: 638). However, strong family values and the resulting trust in many family firms may make fraudulent and dysfunctional behaviors more likely as such firms are unable to control certain family members' pursuit of self-interest rather than the overall good of the firm (Ding & Wu, 2014). One element of this book is examining how these dynamics manifest across family firms, whether previous research addresses if either of these conditions is more dominant, and how future research can inform us regarding this apparent conflict. Within the following chapters, these questions will be asked, and answers to them attempted:

- What leads to dysfunctional and deviant behavior in family firms?
- What types of deviant and dysfunctional behaviors occur in family firms?
- What are the outcomes of deviant and dysfunctional behavior and how do they affect individuals, families, firms, and the external environment? What are the effects of dysfunctional behavior at the individual and family levels on the firm and its internal and external stakeholders—and vice versa?
- What factors make it more or less likely for either family or non-family employees to engage in dysfunctional behavior directed at the family, the family firm, or the external stakeholders?
- What directions might future research take to build on what has been done thus far in researching this crucial topic?

A fundamental conversation in family business scholarship is whether family businesses, which provide a driving force in economic systems around the world, are inherently good or bad due to the family's involvement (Kidwell et al., 2023). On the one hand, some researchers focus on the negative aspects of family firms such as a family's poor treatment of non-family employees, downsides of the principal-principal agency relationship (taking advantage of non-family owners), negative outcomes of favoritism toward family members, an atmosphere of secrecy, and the real presence of organized crime families across the world. On the other hand, research stresses the positive aspects of family firms such as interpersonal trust among family, the development of family capital and family bonds, and the stewardship of the firm, seeing it to the next generation often to the benefit of the community. This divide in perceptions and outcomes in many ways illustrates the antecedents and outcomes due to the heterogeneity of family firms, and it is quite relevant to the focus of this book.

This book is inspired and informed generally by several years of research into the topics of deviance and dysfunction and specifically by two other works, a book chapter on the diversity of deviance (Kidwell et al., 2019) that appeared in Esra Memili's and Clay Dibrell's comprehensive Palgrave Handbook of Heterogeneity among Family Firms, and an ongoing literature review that focuses on dysfunctional behavior in family businesses and is co-authored by Kimberly Eddleston, Linda Kidwell, Jim Cater, and Ellison Howard (Kidwell et al., 2023).

The chapters in this book are presented as follows. Chapter 2 considers the causes of deviance and dysfunction that may start within business families and lead to different outcomes in different family firms. After a discussion of the relevance of theoretical perspectives such as social exchange theory and psychological contract violations, the impact of a perpetrator's personality traits, particularly elements of the Dark Triad, is examined. Next, the ambiguous connection of conflict to deviance and dysfunction is discussed followed by the application of emotions in the family firm context to consider how the seeds of deviance and dysfunction may be sown as altruism and reaped as entitlement. The pursuit of socioemotional wealth is also considered for its role as a potential contributor to dysfunction. Family firm dysfunction is then connected to elements of family science research such as parent–child relationships, parenting style, and sibling relationships. Finally, the influences of the external environment in terms of weak institutions and legal protection, prevalence of corruption, and other factors are linked to the potential for bribery, corruption, and other negative behaviors on the part of the family firm.

Chapter 3 reviews the various types of behaviors that can be deviant, dysfunctional, and damaging, focusing on behaviors that mainly are perpetrated by individuals and groups within the context of the family and the family firm. A brief discussion of major theories used in the research of dysfunctional behaviors in family firms is followed by a review of the specific behaviors that target individuals, the family, and the family firm. These behaviors include family member impediment to the success of the firm manifested through counterproductive work behavior, bullying, theft, withholding information, aggression, resistance to change, bifurcation bias, gender discrimination, and conflicts that have grown from interpersonal disputes into those that involve the broader business. The heterogeneity of the behaviors in this category appears evident in terms of types and potential targets. Yet, it is important to address why there is relatively little research at this level compared to other dysfunctional phenomena studied in a family firm context.

Chapter 4 moves the discussion to focus on a variety of negative behaviors perpetrated by family firm leaders and members and directed outside the firm. These negative acts target and impact the family business's external stakeholders and the business itself. These behaviors include fraud and other financial misconduct including earnings manipulation, bribery/corruption, tax avoidance, tax evasion, and corporate social irresponsibility including negative environmental performance. There is much research in the management, accounting, and finance disciplines in the areas of financial misconduct, earnings management, tax avoidance/evasion, and fraud with researchers focusing on irresponsible behaviors by family firms and their implications. Key differences in the frequency of these behaviors across family firms and their effects—positive and negative—are important questions that are addressed in subsequent chapters.

Chapter 5 considers the impact of these behaviors on individuals, families, family firms, and external stakeholders. Not only firm performance is affected by dysfunctional acts within the family or family firm, but the succession process, the governance process, the firm's reputation, familial relationships, and the interests of external stakeholders can also be damaged. Family firms can be locked into a vicious circle of negative behaviors based upon the way that dysfunctional acts are managed within the firm; a circle that can end in dissolution of the firm and isolation from the family. This chapter also discusses the ambiguity of deviance and dysfunction, how its outcomes can do a family "good" and sometimes a society "bad"—and sometimes benefit both through constructive deviance.

Chapter 6 circles back to antecedents of dysfunction with a major focus on family systems and family science, which are areas that provide rich theoretical ground in which to study how early family relationships can spur deviance and dysfunction in some family firms (Kidwell et al., 2023). In this chapter, it is argued that changing definitions of family and establishment and growth of the family system as well as theories focusing on parental control, family niche-model of birth order and personality, family communication patterns, developmental psychology, and kinship theory can tell more about the roots of bad behavior than has been revealed in previous family business research. Finally, the firm's external context is examined to determine the roles that culture and potentially race and ethnicity play in how bad behavior is viewed and managed in diverse family firms.

The closing Chapter 7 of the book discusses implications of the current picture for future theoretical and empirical work in the heterogeneity of dysfunction and deviance in family firms. Several gaps in the literature are identified based on current research findings and ways forward on several fronts are suggested. In this chapter, research that considers various types of potentially deviant or dysfunctional behavior in family firms is integrated, resulting in a proposed multilevel framework that potentially cuts across individuals, families, firms, and environments. Such a model and additional encouragement to consider a microfoundations theory that links individual behavior to behavior at higher levels of analysis can help guide and organize research in this increasingly diverse area of scholarly and practical concern that transcends academic disciplines. The chapter also suggests that different motivations for committing dysfunctional acts that may hurt the family and the family firm may be found by examining research in other disciplines. Thus, again, multidisciplinary research is suggested as a way forward. Finally, throughout the book, anecdotes relating actual examples of dysfunctional and deviant behavior are used to connect academic research with practical application. These stories illustrate many of the behaviors that have been studied in scholarly work and are designed to make the concepts discussed in the text more salient and accessible to the reader.

References

Aguilera, R. V., Judge, W. Q., & Terjesen, S. A. (2018). Corporate governance deviance. *Academy of Management Review*, *43*(1), 87–109.

Astrachan, J. H., Binz, C., Campopiano, G., & Baù, M. (2020). Values, spirituality, and religion: Family business and the roots of sustainable ethical behavior. *Journal of Business Ethics, 163*(4), 637–645.

Bennett, R. J., & Robinson, S. L. (2000). Development of a measure of workplace deviance. *Journal of applied psychology*, *85*(3), 349–360.

Chua, J. H., Chrisman, J. J., & Sharma, P. (1999). Defining the family business by behavior. *Entrepreneurship Theory and Practice*, *23*(4), 19–39.

Daspit, J. J., Chrisman, J. J., Ashton, T., & Evangelopoulos, N. (2021). Family firm heterogeneity: A definition, common themes, scholarly progress, and directions forward. *Family Business Review*, *34*(3), 296–322.

De Massis, A., Kotlar, J., & Manelli, L. (2021). Family firms, family boundary organizations, and the family-related organizational ecosystem. *Family Business Review, 34*(4), 350–364.

Diaz-Moriana, V., Hogan, T., Clinton, E., & Brophy, M. (2019). Defining family business: A closer look at definitional heterogeneity. In E. Memili & C. Dibrell (Eds.), *The Palgrave handbook of heterogeneity among family firms* (pp. 333–374).

Ding, S., Qu, B., & Wu, Z. (2016). Family control, socioemotional wealth, and governance environment: The case of bribes. *Journal of Business Ethics, 136*(3), 639–654.

Ding, S., & Wu, Z. (2014). Family ownership and corporate misconduct in U.S. small firms. *Journal of Business Ethics, 123*(2), 183–195.

Eddleston, K., & Mulki, J. (2021). Differences in family-owned SMEs' ethical behavior: A mixed gamble perspective of family firm tax evasion. *Entrepreneurship Theory and Practice, 45*(4), 767–791.

Giacalone, R. A., & Greenberg, J. (1997). *Antisocial behavior in organizations.* Sage.

Gomez-Mejia, L. R., Haynes, K. T., Nunez-Nickel, M., Jacobson, K. J. L., & Moyano-Fuentes, J. (2007). Socioemotional wealth and business risks in family-controlled firms: Evidence from Spanish olive oil mills. *Administrative Science Quarterly, 52*, 106–137.

Griffin, R. W., & Lopez, Y. P. (2005). "Bad behavior" in organizations: A review and typology for future research. *Journal of Management, 31*(6), 988–1005.

Griffin, R. W., O'Leary-Kelly, A. & Collins, J. M. (1998). *Dysfunctional behavior in organizations: Violent and deviant behavior. Monographs in organizational behavior and industrial relations* (Vol. 23). JAI Press.

Jaskiewicz, P., Uhlenbruck, K., Balkin, D. B., & Reay, T. (2013). Is nepotism good or bad? Types of nepotism and implications for knowledge management. *Family Business Review, 26*(2), 121–139.

Kidwell, R. E., Cox, K. C., & Kloepfer, K. E. (2019). The diversity of deviance: How it can hurt (and help) families and family firms. *The Palgrave handbook of heterogeneity among family firms* (pp. 643–672).

Kidwell, R. E., Eddleston, K. A., Kidwell, L. A., Cater III, J. J. & Howard, E. (2023). *Dysfunctional behavior in family firms across individuals, families, firms, and environments* (Unpublished working paper).

Kidwell, R. E., Kellermanns, F. W., & Eddleston, K. A. (2012). Harmony, justice, confusion and conflict in the family firm: Implications for ethical climate and the "Fredo effect." *Journal of Business Ethics,* 106, 503–517.

Kidwell, R. E., & Nygaard, A. (2011). A strategic deviance perspective on the franchise form of organizing. *Entrepreneurship Theory & Practice*, 35(3), 467–482.

Latané, B., Williams, K., & Harkins, S. (1979). Many hands make light the work: The causes and consequences of social loafing. *Journal of Personality and Social Psychology, 37* (6), 822.

Lin, B., Mainemelis, C. & Kark, R. 2016. Leaders' responses to creative deviance: Differential effects on subsequent creative deviance and creative performance, *The Leadership Quarterly*, 27, 537–556.

Locke, E. A. (2003). Good definitions: The epistemological foundation of scientific progress. In J. Greenberg (Ed.), *Organizational behavior: The state of the science* (2nd ed., pp. 415–444). Lawrence Erlbaum.

Mackey, J. D., McAllister, C. P., Ellen, B. P., III., & Carson, J. E. (2021). A meta-analysis of interpersonal and organizational workplace deviance research. *Journal of Management, 47*, 597–622.

Madison, K., Daspit, J., Turner, K., & Kellermanns, F. (2018). Family firm human resource practices: Investigating the effects of professionalization and bifurcation bias on performance. *Journal of Business Research, 84*, 327–336.

Mainemelis, C. (2010). Stealing fire: Creative deviance in the evolution of new ideas. *Academy of Management Review*, 35, 558–578.

Marcus, B., Taylor, O. A., Hastings, S. E., Sturm, A., & Weigelt, O. (2016). The structure of counterproductive work behavior: A review, a structural meta-analysis, and a primary study. *Journal of Management*, *42*(1), 203–233.

Merton, R. K. (1957). Social structure and anomie. In R. K. Merton (Ed.), *Social theory and social structure* (pp. 185–214). The Free Press.

O'Brien, K. E., Minjock, R. M., Colarelli, S. M., & Yang, C. (2018). Kinship ties and employee theft perceptions in family-owned businesses. *European Management Journal, 36*(3), 421–430.

Rau, S. B., Schneider-Siebke, V., & Günther, C. (2019). Family firm values explaining family firm heterogeneity. *Family Business Review, 32*(2), 195–215.

Robinson, S. L., & Bennett, R. J. (1995). A typology of deviant workplace behaviors: A multidimensional scaling study. *Academy of Management Journal, 38*(2), 555–572.

Spector, P. E., Fox, S., Penney, L. M., Bruursema, K., Goh, A., & Kessler, S. (2006). The dimensionality of counter productivity: Are all counterproductive behaviors created equal? *Journal of Vocational Behavior*, *68*(3), 446–460.

Spreitzer, G. M., & Sonenshein, S. (2004). Toward the construct definition of positive deviance. *American Behavioral Scientist, 47*, 828–847.

Swab, R. G., Sherlock, C., Markin, E., & Dibrell, C. (2020). "SEW" What do we know and where do we go? A review of socioemotional wealth and a way forward. *Family Business Review, 33*(4), 424–445.

Tagiuri, R., & Davis, J. (1992). On the goals of successful family corporations. *Family Business Review,* 5, 43–62.

Temouri, Y., Nardella, G., Jones, C., & Brammer, S. (2022). Haven-sent? Tax havens, corporate social irresponsibility and the dark side of family firm internationalization. *British Journal of Management*, *33*(3), 1447–1467.
Vadera, A. K., Pratt, M. G. & Mishra, P. (2013). Constructive deviance in organizations: Integrating and moving forward. *Journal of Management*, *39*, 1221–1276.
Vardi, Y., & Weitz, E. (2004). *Misbehavior in organizations: Theory, research, and management*. Lawrence Erlbaum Associates.

CHAPTER 2

Antecedents of Dysfunction and Deviance in the Family Firm

Abstract The various causes of deviance and dysfunction usually start with interactions that occurred between individuals, the family, and the family firm and lead to diverse outcomes in different family firms. After discussing theoretical perspectives such as social exchange theory and psychological contract violations, this chapter considers the impact of a perpetrator's personality traits, particularly elements of the Dark Triad, on dysfunctional behavior. Then, the ambiguity of conflict's relationship to deviance and dysfunction is discussed followed by applications of emotion, altruism, entitlement, and nepotism in the family firm context, which can serve as antecedents to deviance and dysfunction. The positive and negative effects of socioemotional wealth are also discussed. Family firm dysfunction is connected to elements of family science research such as parent–child relationships, parenting style, and sibling relationships. Finally, the influences of the external environment in terms of weak institutions and legal protections, prevalence of corruption, and other factors are linked to the potential for bribery, corruption, and other negative behaviors on the part of the family firm.

Keywords Relationship conflict · Social exchange · Psychological contract · Dark Triad · Nepotism · Altruism · Socioemotional wealth · Family relationships · Family firms

R. E. Kidwell, *Dysfunction and Deviance Across Family Firms*, Palgrave Studies in Family Business Heterogeneity,
https://doi.org/10.1007/978-3-031-51816-4_2

> Well, we're important to each other until we start fighting and then all the love suddenly doesn't exist anymore, I think that's commonly what you will see. Now, I'm not suggesting that's happened to me in my family because I'm always a peacemaker. I'm the one who can come in and say, right, let's break this up. You get on your side, and you get on your side, and I'm going to help you fix this, and they'll, you know, either do that or won't and then I'll go, well I tried. But I'm not choosing sides here when they're in the heart of that, right? And I think they literally hate each other in that moment, you can feel it. You can tell that they never want to speak again and they're never going to forgive each other. And when they started the brainchild of the business, they loved each other and couldn't wait to work with each other. Everybody was agreeable until the disagreements happened.—Family business member discussing conflict within her family firm (Interviewed by author, June 2020)

The vast research on conflict in the business family and the family business tells us that, just like in most instances, conflict can be positive or negative depending on the nature of the conflict and how it is managed (Bettinelli et al., 2022; Kellermanns & Eddleston, 2004, 2007). But when it gets personal and emotional, it leads the way to bad behavior. Conflict is highlighted in this chapter because it is one of the key antecedents in the development of dysfunction and deviance in many family firms. Coupled with childhood family relationships that can set the tone for much later negative acts including those that occur in a family business setting, conflict in relationships can lead to the breaking of norms and behaviors that harm individuals, the family, and the family firm.

In this chapter, conflict and other potential antecedents of dysfunctional and deviant behaviors such as personality (specifically the Dark Triad); family firm characteristics and the effects of altruism, entitlement, and pursuit of socioemotional wealth; formative family relationships; and the influence of the external environment are discussed. Variables such as the dominant national culture (Samara et al., 2021), the nature of the competitive environment (Miller et al., 2003), the effectiveness of a firm's board of directors (Corten et al., 2017), and the degree to which a family firm has professionalized its human resources function (Madison et al., 2018) have been proposed by researchers as potential antecedents of negative behaviors such as bias against non-family members (bifurcation bias), discrimination based on gender, and disputes at the firm level. The degree to which these internal and external precursors of potentially adverse actions are present in the firm and its environment can provide clues as to why serious dysfunction develops in some family firms and in others very little.

2.1 Conceptual Relationships

Before discussing the specific antecedents to dysfunctional behavior in family firms, it is relevant to set the stage by reviewing the concept of social exchange, a paradigm that underlies much of the recent research on individuals and groups in organizations (Cropanzano et al., 2017). Homans (1958) defined social exchange as tangible or intangible activity between at least two people in which the rewards and the costs of the exchange are measured and then serve as the basis for future exchange. Cropanzano et al. (2017) stated that the common elements of more recent models of the social exchange process involve one person (an actor) treating another (a target) positively or negatively (an initiating action) then the target responding to the actor in a positive or negative way (reciprocating responses). The theory predicts that "in reaction to positive initiating actions, targets will tend to reply in kind by engaging in more positive reciprocating responses and/ or fewer negative reciprocating responses" (Cropanzano et al., 2017: 480).

Social exchange models have been applied to many elements of the supervisor-employee relationship as well as to familial relations (e.g., Beckman-Brindley & Tavormina, 1978), the succession process in family firms (Daspit et al., 2016), and the legitimacy of nepotism (Hudson et al., 2019; Jaskiewicz et al., 2013). Yet, the general nature and applicability of social exchange indicate that it is one of many principles that could be used to explain specific relationships between different sets of organizational phenomena that involve tangible or intangible exchanges between two of more people (Cropanzano et al., 2017), e.g., antecedents and behaviors that are dysfunctional and deviant.

Psychological contract is another concept that is worthwhile to discuss here because along with social exchange it can be used to explain the relationship between a dysfunctional behavior and the reasons why it occurs. Psychological contracts involve unwritten reciprocal obligations between an individual and an organization consisting of individual beliefs that in changing conditions important commitments will be fulfilled without having to be part of a written agreement (Rousseau, 1989). A social exchange model that incorporated elements of the psychological contract was tested in family firms, finding that an organization's obligations are antecedents of an individual employee's contributions to firm performance. When family firms met what was expected of them by their employees, the employees met their perceived obligations to their employers (Madden et al., 2017). Considering the "umbrella" of conduct that these two concepts provide is important considering the differential impact that the following antecedents have on behavior within the family and the family firm.

2.2 Interpersonal Conflict

Conflict is a key research topic that has attracted the interest of family firm scholars to the extent that diverse, multiple literature reviews on the subject have been conducted. These reviews have focused on intrafamily conflict (Kubíček & Machek, 2020), conflict management (Alderson, 2015; Caputo et al., 2018), conflict and cohesion in social relationships (Bettinelli et al., 2022), business-related conflicts (Frank et al., 2011), family-related conflicts (Qiu & Freel, 2020), and conflict involving non-family members (Rosecká & Machek, 2022).

Three general types of conflict have been identified in the literature and applied to the study of family firms (Jehn, 1995; Kellermanns & Eddleston, 2007; Loignon et al., 2017). Task conflict relates to disagreements among family members over what tasks should be completed, process conflict involves how work should be accomplished or how and what skills of family members should be used in the workplace to complete those tasks, and relationship conflict involves high-emotion personal animosities among family members (Jehn & Mannix, 2001; Kellermanns & Eddleston, 2004). The first two types of conflict—task and process—can potentially improve family firm performance (Kellermanns & Eddleston, 2004, 2007). If channeled properly, disagreements over the family firm's long-term goals, its business model, and the firm's procedures for effective succession can inspire more effective solutions to serious issues facing the family and the firm. Likewise, the family firm leadership, i.e., the dominant coalition, may also disagree with family members and each other as to how the goals and strategies they agree on should be accomplished or implemented. For example, Alexandra, the family firm CEO, may wish for her nephew Toby, a next generation family member, to focus on growing the firm's marketing function, while her sister Sally, another family firm executive and Toby's mother, may contend that he would do better in an operations role. If this process conflict results in Toby being assigned to the most appropriate position in the family business, the firm achieves a benefit from the disagreement.

However, if conflicts over what to do and how to do it are personal, in that they are either based on previous personal animus or on interpersonal conflicts among family members, the stage is set for future dysfunction. If Toby is assigned to marketing against his will, he may become emotional, take it personally, and engage in negative behaviors to act out his resentment against Alexandra. Or it may be that Sally has a long-standing conflict with Alexandra based on past events and only opposes Toby's marketing assignment because she does not get along with her sister. These types of relationship conflicts are unique to family firms in that they can spill over into the firm from the family or vice versa (Kellermanns & Eddleston, 2007). The degree to which a family firm suffers strong relationship conflicts among its leaders and members will have different results regarding the level of deviance and dysfunction exhibited by its members (Eddleston & Kellermanns, 2007). Escalation of family fights damages the warring family members and negatively impacts shareholder value as they result in serious dysfunctions that can feed back into the original conflicts and amplify them; these feuds and their impact on dysfunction are well documented (Gordon & Nicholson, 2008) and a global phenomenon as well (*Economist*, 2021; Hunt, 2012).

2.3 Personality—The Dark Triad

The impact of the personal characteristics of the leadership of a family firm and its members differs across organizations based on the degree to which negative elements of personality are revealed in the family business's dominant coalition. Three important aspects of personality have the potential to set the stage for dysfunction in a family business. This "Dark Triad" consists of narcissism, Machiavellianism, and psychopathy (Paulhus & Williams, 2002). Subsequently, Paulhus (2014) added a fourth, everyday sadism, characterized by enjoyment of cruelty, and linked it to subsequent bullying of others.

Thus far, the limited focus of family business researchers has been on the first three types, all of which involve individuals pursuing self-interested goals (McLarty & Holt, 2019). Narcissists display callousness and grandiosity to obtain the admiration of others, which feeds into a deep desire to create and maintain a positive view of themselves (Galvin et al., 2015; McLarty & Holt, 2019; Paulhus, 2014). Machiavellians attempt to control others through manipulation to further their own agenda and to attain personal goals, often at the heartless expense of others (Liyanagamage et al., 2023; Paulhus, 2014). Psychopaths are those who bring harm to others impulsively, often through manipulation, and seek to gain personal gratification at the expense of building relationships (Paulhus, 2014; Williams et al., 2007). Motivations for each type to behave unethically include personal benefit (narcissism), deception (Machiavellianism), and rationalization (psychopathy) (Harrison et al., 2018). Although Machiavellians are drawn to engage in white-collar crime, psychopathy is the only one of the original three dark traits that can be characterized in the extreme by criminal behavior (Paulhus, 2014).

A classic example of a psychopath with family business connections was Bernard Madoff who was turned into the FBI by his sons—both worked for the legitimate arm of his firm—for masterminding a $65 billion Ponzi scheme that resulted in one of the biggest investment frauds in Wall Street history (History.com Editors, 2011). Madoff paid his earlier investors with funds received from more recent investors. This left many of the latter to lose the life savings they had entrusted to Madoff when the scam fell apart during the 2008 financial crisis as the earlier clients took out more money than he could bring in from newer clients to cover the withdrawals. Madoff, who was convicted and died in prison, illustrates the effects of psychopathic leadership on illegal practices such as fraud in the financial sector and is an example of findings that support the view that corporate psychopaths can be found in senior roles in the financial services sector (Boddy, 2023), and the family firm.

Recognizing that elements of the Dark Triad exist in varying degrees within individuals as well as groups, families, and firms can account for differences in the level of impact that narcissism, Machiavellianism, and psychopathy have on deviant and dysfunctional behavior in family firms. Recent research notwithstanding, study of the triad's impact has been limited in entrepreneurship and family business research (Klotz & Neubaum, 2016; McLarty et al., 2023). It is important in family business settings to examine how these elements of personality interact with other potential antecedents present in the family and the firm: conflict, as has been discussed, and context, which is elaborated on next.

2.4 Family Firm Context

Within family firms, several questions arise that have implications for whether there is higher likelihood for subsequent dysfunctional and deviant behavior to occur in certain firms versus others. Grouped within the family firm context are potential antecedents of dysfunction that include whether merit-based or need-based rewards for family members dominate, and the degree to which engagement in asymmetric altruism by a family firm leader, a parent for example, leads to a sense of entitlement on the part of a family firm member (Eddleston & Kidwell, 2012). The family firm's dominant coalition's stance toward nepotism as a matter of policy or practice in hiring and promoting family members is another contingency to be examined as is the way the family pursues its non-economic goals. Each of these factors plays a role in increasing (or reducing) the likelihood of dysfunction occurring in a particular family.

The question of whether rewards provided to family members are based on merit versus need is a key element in defining the family firm and has strong connections to the development of potential dysfunctional behavior in the family firm (Eddleston & Kidwell, 2012). Family firms are often regarded in terms of whether the business or the family comes first (Poza, 2013). The implication is the business-first case indicates family members are rewarded based on meritorious performance; the family-first case suggests that family member needs and desires for equality trump merit as the basis for distributing rewards. The orientation and execution of the reward system can stir high negative emotions, split families, lead to relationship conflict, and ultimately cause damage to some firms more than others due to the negative actions that are discussed in the following chapter.

Asymmetric (one-sided) altruism and feelings of entitlement and unfairness come into play as potential causes of dysfunction in the case of family firm leaders who are overly generous toward their employed children, thus encouraging them not to fulfill their responsibilities to the business and to stay dependent on the parents (Schulze et al., 2001). This can create major incentives for some children to expect their parents to provide resources for them despite a lack of performance, encouraging deviance and dysfunction in the family firm. Parents, however, don't see the issue in the same way as does a detached observer and continue to provide for the undeserving child. This leads to more of the same damaging behavior from the children who continue it because they see no consequences for their actions or lack thereof (Lubatkin et al., 2005; Van den Berghe & Carchon, 2003). The "silver spoon syndrome" (Hollander, 2002) leads parents not to correct children who undermine the family firm or otherwise underperform, showing themselves to be ill-suited to the family business. These individuals are protected due to the blind faith of the parents who continue their altruistic behavior, which from a strategic perspective has become costly stewardship to the family firm (Miller et al., 2013).

However, altruism may breed a sense of entitlement in some children but not others, indicating that generous altruistic parenting is not necessarily the issue per se. Rather, it is generous altruistic parents who reward based on needs and wants and not merit that indicates differential impact from firm to firm. Feelings of injustice are unique in this situation as family members compare themselves to other relatives based on family status as well as status at work. Fairness norms in the family domain focus largely on equality, with each family member getting an equal share of opportunities and resources regardless of merit, although merit based on performance must be the driving norm in the business domain.

The discussion of altruism, entitlement, and fairness leads to consideration of nepotism policies and practices in family firms as a potential cause of dysfunction. Nepotism in a family firm occurs when its family members are more favorably treated than non-family members in hiring, promotion, and other job elements (Bellow, 2003; Jaskiewicz et al., 2013). Nepotism practices have also been considered an antecedent of dysfunctional behavior because they raise perceptions of injustice and bias against non-family employees (Collin & Ahlberg, 2012; Spranger et al., 2012). The term carries a negative connotation because the implication is often that the favored family member is not deserving of the job but benefits from an entitlement. However, the business family may favor hiring and promoting the firm's family members to ensure that family values are preserved, and that nepotism helps perpetuate stewardship of the family business (Jaskiewicz et al., 2013; Jeong et al., 2022). Yet, if non-family employees perceive they are being treated unfairly, they may believe the psychological contract has been violated due to unjust entitlements being afforded to family members and address this perceived injustice by engaging in negative work behaviors (Ward et al., 2007).

Socioemotional wealth (SEW) consists of non-economic goals that add emotional value to the firm and the family (Gomez-Mejia et al.,

2007) such as passionate connection to and control of the family business, transgenerational succession, and reputation (Berrone et al., 2012). The pursuit of SEW has been identified as an antecedent of dysfunctional behavior in some family firms (Fehre & Weber, 2019; Kellermanns et al., 2012; Zientara, 2017). SEW provides a conceptual perspective to explain dysfunction inside the firm, e.g., bifurcation bias (Samara et al., 2021), and dysfunction outside the firm, e.g., corporate social irresponsibility (Cabeza-Garcia et al., 2017). However, the pursuit of SEW to enhance the family's identity, continuity, and influence has long been recognized as a positive force (Swab et al., 2020), even to the extent that it can lessen the likelihood of dysfunctional behavior in family firms (e.g., McLarty & Holt, 2019). Thus, SEW serves as an example of a concept that can have both positive and/or negative impacts on dysfunction and deviance depending upon how the family seeks to achieve its non-economic goals.

2.5 Early Family Relationships

> It is believed that a parent will directly affect deviant behavior through parenting and the family structure, while indirectly affecting the behaviors through the adolescent's community, and their choice of peers. (Carlson, 2012: 42)

> When he was growing up, my grandpa was best friends with his older sister. They did EVERYTHING together. One day, his sister had a friend over, and my grandpa went to go play with them. His sister said something along the lines of 'Don't follow us, we don't want to play with boys' or something to that effect. It sounds silly and childish, but that hurt my grandpa so badly that it changed their relationship completely. He instead turned to becoming best friends with their younger brother and that dynamic has stayed even to this day. (Buzzfeed, 2023)

The differential impact of parent–child interactions, sibling relationships, and other elements of growing from child to adult cannot be underestimated in terms of their connections to future behavior within the family firm. Parent–child relationships are a key element in this process in that some parents view and treat their children differently in terms of how they exercise control and how they may favor one child over another. Parents who practice favoritism with their children place them in either an ingroup or an outgroup, foreshadowing later preferential treatment when they join the family business and provoking dysfunctional behavior by offspring who see themselves as less favored (Cater et al., 2016; Eddleston & Kidwell, 2012). In addition, research indicates that roles children adopt as they engage with family and grow into adolescence and adulthood have an impact later in life (Sanders et al., 2014). These identified roles include hero, scapegoat, lost child, mascot, caretaker, and mastermind (Sanders et al., 2014; Zagefka et al., 2021). Researchers specializing in family therapy tested how these roles related to family dysfunction and the likelihood that depressive symptoms for the role taker would occur later in life; they found that children in dysfunctional families were more likely to take on the difficult roles of scapegoat and lost child, and the children in those roles had more symptoms of depression in adulthood (Zagefka et al., 2021).

In families that own and operate businesses, segmenting the family role and the workplace role is extremely challenging (Cooper et al., 2013). When the family role has become a problematic one, perhaps due to the dysfunctional nature of the family, it might be expected that this becomes an antecedent of further negative behaviors within a family firm. The scapegoat child is the target of blame and shame for everything that goes wrong in the family and illustrates an extreme example of a disfavored child (Pillari, 1991). The child cast in the role of scapegoat can develop guilt and a negative self-image that is destructive to the individual, the family, and the family firm (Kidwell et al., 2019). On the other hand, children cast as heroes and master minds by their parents or siblings may display more positive than negative behaviors when they join the family firm. Yet, they may also develop a sense of entitlement due to being cast in the role of favored child.

Parent–child relationships are important to the development of later bad behavior in other ways as well; one of these is how parents control their offspring. In parental control theory, three dominant parenting styles have differential impacts on the characteristics of their children to the extent they were self-reliant, trusting, content, or likely heading toward delinquency (Baumrind, 1967, 1971; Brauer, 2017; Harris-McKoy, 2016). The three styles (authoritarian, authoritative, and permissive) affect how children behave as adults as well as how they treat other family members in the context of the family business, thus providing another source of heterogeneity. A demanding, yet kind, (authoritative) parenting style generally produces content, self-controlled, self-reliant children. On the other hand, authoritarian parents whose style is detached, controlling and less warm than other parents have children who are relatively discontent, withdrawn, and distrustful. Permissive-style parents, who are not demanding or controlling but relatively warm, produce children who are the least self-controlled, explorative, and reliant (Baumrind, 1971). These differences lead to the issue of whether some parenting styles raise rebels and others cultivate conformists (Brauer, 2017). Results of one parental control study suggest that too much or too little parental control is related to higher delinquent behavior (Harris-McKoy, 2016).

Parent–child relationships can influence a variety of elements within the child including acceptance of the parents' values and the child's moral development (Laible & Thompson, 2000). Children in weak parent–child relationships show less self-restraint than children in stronger relationships (Laible & Thompson, 2000) and have more behavior problems (Richmond & Stocker, 2008). Thus, a family with weak parent–child relationships influences future anti-social behavior by children when they become adults (Bullock et al., 2002).

Sibling relationships, such as described in the anecdote above regarding grandpa and his sister, provide another area where differences and potentially disputes that occur early in life are projected into adulthood. A perceived slight or rejection that occurred early on can trigger perceptions and behaviors well into adulthood. Siblings who fought over toys as children continue to battle as they grow older, culminating in serious and negative behaviors after entering the family firm. One family member shared that after he accidentally knocked his older brother down the stairs at a sporting event when he was a pre-teen, he suspected his brother had viewed him negatively ever since. Family differences in terms of disagreements spilling over from initial family interactions are a source of dysfunctional behavior with extremely negative consequences for the family and the firm (Cater et al., 2016).

Connections made from the business family to family therapy, family psychology, and family science (e.g., Combs et al., 2020) reveal a ripe area for research into differential impacts on family firms from interplay with family issues. Whether the issue is parental control of the children, family communications, sibling tensions, or role development, insights from the family science, family therapy and family psychology literatures have shown promise in predicting the occurrence of dysfunctional behavior in family firms (Eddleston & Kidwell, 2012; Huang et al., 2020; Shanine et al., 2023). Chapter 6 will consider the topic of early family relationships and their differential impacts on dysfunction in greater detail.

2.6 Environmental Influences

Most of the discussion thus far has been on the differential effects of antecedents in dysfunctional acts that occur within the firm such as counterproductive work behavior, bullying, and bifurcation bias. Yet, it is also important to consider the role that environmental influences play regarding deviant and dysfunctional behavior that is directed outside the firm such as fraud, financial manipulation, bribery, corruption, and tax evasion. These antecedents include an environment that features weak institutions, weak legal protections, poor economic conditions, and an atmosphere of pervasive corruption (private gain resulting from abuse of power). In examining previous research into external dysfunction, a key consensus regarding negative behaviors such as bribery and corruption by family firms is that these acts result largely from environmental conditions that support such behavior (Kidwell et al., 2023).

For example, previous research has investigated how family firms and their leaders behave when there is a lack of legal protection of property rights in certain countries (Tang et al., 2013), weaknesses in a country's governance mechanisms (Ding et al., 2016), and in highly corrupt settings (Bassetti et al., 2015; Yamanoi & Asaba, 2018). Researchers have also studied differences across family firms, such as the impact of founder presence (Brune et al., 2019), family involvement (Sanchez-Marin et al., 2016), a business's political connections (Du, 2015), and a firm's performance (Cruz et al., 2014; Eddleston & Mulki, 2021) on the likelihood that family businesses would commit negative acts directed toward external stakeholders. Recently, Purkayastha and colleagues (2022) examined how the heterogeneity of a family business's internal governance mechanisms impacted both principal-agent and principal-principal agency conflicts when faced with a less developed institutional environment, finding that the combination of a family's concentrated ownership position along with the family's management control could have different effects on agency conflicts in the family business.

Taken as a whole, these studies indicate growing research interest in how external environmental conditions may drive families and family firms either toward or away from behaviors that hurt the firm as well as damage external stakeholders. Finally, it is also important to clarify that the external antecedents discussed here could have an impact on dysfunctional behavior inside the firm, and the internal antecedents discussed earlier could affect behavior outside the firm. For example, external economic conditions could inspire employee theft just as Dark Triad personality traits could lead to financial fraud of clients.

2.7 Concluding Comments

This chapter indicates that conflict, personality, context, family relationships, and the external environment act as antecedents that can lead to deviant and dysfunctional behavior within a family firm or in its external environment. The origin of these antecedents, examples of what potential behaviors they entail, and potentially positive as well as negative outcomes are noted in Table 2.1.

The next chapters illustrate in more detail the types of behaviors that may result and their impact on the family and the family business. As noted, conflict is usually seen as negative, but it can be positive depending on the type of conflict, how it is managed, interests of the different family members involved, and their levels of emotion. This is true of other concepts that have been the focus of family business research. For example, a cohesive family can work well together due to the bonds that have been nurtured over time, yet high cohesiveness can lead to premature consensus, groupthink, and poor decision making as family leaders rush to judgment (Bettinelli et al., 2022). The ambiguity of how intentions and circumstances interact tends to provide different results in linking antecedents with behaviors that may help or hurt the family, the firm, and its stakeholders.

Table 2.1 Antecedents of deviance/dysfunction and potential behaviors and effects

Antecedents	*Potential behavior*	*Potential positive*	*Potential negative*
Conflict			
Task	Problem solving	Goal clarity	Suboptimal solutions
Process	Problem solving	Smooth operations	Lack of buy-in
Relationship	Family fighting	Few, if any	Dysfunctional behavior
Personality			
Dark Triad	Pursuit of Self-interested goals	Dominant crisis leader	Manipulation, control, dysfunction
Firm context			
Rewards	Need or merit distribution	Perceived fairness and motivation	Perceived injustice
Altruism	Undeserved rewards lead to entitlement	Family relations continue	Dysfunctional behaviors continue and escalate
Nepotism	Bias in favor of family	Stewardship of the firm	Non-family discrimination, perceived injustice
SEW pursuit	Achieve non-economic goals	Family firm identity, reputation boost	Corporate irresponsibility, damage to reputation due to zealous pursuit
Family relations			
Parent–child relations	Role making of children	Hero—does everything right	Scapegoat—responsible for anything that goes wrong
Parenting style	How children are "parented"	Confident talented adults	Distrustful adults who lack self-control
Siblings	Rivalry	Healthy competition	Unhealthy long-term issues
Environment			
Weak institutions	Engage in illegal acts bribery	Possible short-term gain	Family firm destroyed through illegal behavior
Widespread corruption	Engage in corruption	Possible short-term gain	Family firm destroyed through illegal behavior
Outside shareholders	Take unfair advantage Re-design structure	Successful governance mechanisms	Stakeholder mistreatment, legal issues

References

Alderson, K. (2015). Conflict management and resolution in family-owned businesses: A practitioner focused review. *Journal of Family Business Management, 5*(2), 140–156.

Bassetti, T., Maso, L., & Lattanzi, N. (2015). Family businesses in Eastern European countries: How informal payments affect exports. *Journal of Family Business Strategy, 6*, 219–233.

Baumrind, D. (1967). Child care practices anteceding three patterns of preschool behavior. *Genetic Psychology Monographs, 75*, 43–88.

Baumrind, D. (1971). Current patterns of parental authority. *Developmental Psychology, 4*, 1–103.

Beckman-Brindley, S., & Tavormina, J. B. (1978). Power relationships in families: A social-exchange perspective. *Family Process, 17*(4), 423–436.

Bellow, A. (2003). *In praise of nepotism*. Random House.

Berrone, P., Cruz, C., & Gómez-Mejía, L. R. (2012). Socioemotional wealth in family firms: Theoretical dimensions, assessment approaches, and agenda for future research. *Family Business Review, 25*(3), 258–279.

Bettinelli, C., Mismetti, M., De Massis, A., & Del Bosco, B. (2022). A review of conflict and cohesion in social relationships in family firms. *Entrepreneurship Theory and Practice, 46*, 539–577.

Boddy, C. R. (2023). Insights into the Bernie Madoff financial market scandal which identify new opportunities for business market researchers. *International Journal of Market Research*. https://doi.org/10.1177/14707853231173260

Brauer, J. R. (2017). Cultivating conformists or raising rebels? Connecting parental control and autonomy support to adolescent delinquency. *Journal of Research on Adolescence, 27*(2), 452–470.

Brune, A., Thomsen, M., & Watrin, C. (2019). Family firm heterogeneity and tax avoidance: The role of the founder. *Family Business Review, 32*(3), 296–317.

Bullock, B. M., Bank, L., & Burraston, B. (2002). Adult sibling expressed emotion and fellow sibling deviance: A new piece of the family process puzzle. *Journal of Family Psychology, 16*(3), 307–317.

Buzzfeed. (2023, August 23). *People are sharing the scandal that nearly (or fully) tore their family apart, and some of these make "Succession" look tame*. https://www.yahoo.com/lifestyle/people-revealing-scandal-nearly-tore-034604626.html. Accessed October 16, 2023.

Cabeza-Garcia, L., Sacristan-Navarro, M., & Gomez-Anson, S. (2017). Family involvement and corporate social responsibility disclosure. *Journal of Family Business Strategy, 9*, 109–122.

Caputo, A., Marzi, G., Pellegrini, M. M., & Rialti, R. (2018). Conflict management in family businesses: A bibliometric analysis and systematic literature review. *International Journal of Conflict Management, 29*(4), 519–542.

Carlson, A. (2012). How parents influence deviant behavior among adolescents: An analysis of their family life, community, and peers. *Perspectives, 4*(1), 42–51.

Cater, J. J., III., Kidwell, R. E., & Camp, K. M. (2016). Successor team dynamics in family firms. *Family Business Review, 29*(3), 301–326.

Collin, S. O. Y., & Ahlberg, J. (2012). Blood in the boardroom: Family relationships influencing the functions of the board. *Journal of Family Business Strategy, 3*(4), 207–219.

Combs, J. G., Shanine, K. K., Burrows, S., Allen, J. S., & Pounds, T. W. (2020). What do we know about business families? Setting the stage for leveraging family science theories. *Family Business Review, 33*(1), 38–63.

Cooper, J. T., Kidwell, R. E., & Eddleston, K. A. (2013). Boss and parent, employee and child: Work-family roles and deviant behavior in the family firm. *Family Relations, 62*(3), 457–471.

Corten, M., Steijvers, T., & Lybaert, N. (2017). The effect of intrafamily agency conflicts on audit demand in private family firms: The moderating role of the board of directors. *Journal of Family Business Strategy, 8*, 13–28.

Cropanzano, R., Anthony, E. L., Daniels, S. R., & Hall, A. V. (2017). Social exchange theory: A critical review with theoretical remedies. *Academy of Management Annals, 11*(1), 479–516.

Cruz, C., Larraza-Kintana, M., Garces-Galdeano, L., & Berrone, P. (2014). Are family firms really more socially responsible? *Entrepreneurship Theory and Practice, 38*(6), 1295–1316.

Daspit, J. J., Holt, D. T., Chrisman, J. J., & Long, R. G. (2016). Examining family firm succession from a social exchange perspective: A multiphase, multistakeholder review. *Family Business Review, 29*(1), 44–64.

Ding, S., Qu, B., & Wu, Z. (2016). Family control, socioemotional wealth, and governance environment: The case of bribes. *Journal of Business Ethics, 136*(3), 639–654.

Du, X. (2015). Is corporate philanthropy used as environmental misconduct dressing? Evidence from Chinese family-owned firms. *Journal of Business Ethics, 129*, 341–361.

Economist. (2021, January 30). The surprising role of family feuds in German business. https://www.economist.com/business/2021/01/30/the-surprising-role-of-family-feuds-in-german-business. Accessed October 15, 2023.

Eddleston, K. A., & Kellermanns, F. W. (2007). Destructive and productive family relationships: A stewardship theory perspective. *Journal of Business Venturing, 22*(4), 545–565.

Eddleston, K. A., & Kidwell, R. E. (2012). Parent–child relationships: Planting the seeds of deviant behavior in the family firm. *Entrepreneurship Theory and Practice, 36*(2), 369–386.

Eddleston, K., & Mulki, J. (2021). Differences in family-owned SMEs' ethical behavior: A mixed gamble perspective of family firm tax evasion. *Entrepreneurship Theory and Practice, 45*(4), 767–791.

Fehre, K., & Weber, F. (2019). Why some are more equal: Family firm heterogeneity and the effect on management's attention to CSR. *Business Ethics: A European Review, 28*(3), 321–334.

Frank, H., Kessler, A., Nosé, L., & Suchy, D. (2011). Conflicts in family firms: State of the art and perspectives for future research. *Journal of Family Business Management, 1*(2), 130–153.

Galvin, B. M., Lange, D., & Ashforth, B. E. (2015). Narcissistic organizational identification: Seeing oneself as central to the organization's identity. *Academy of Management Review, 40*(2), 163–181.

Gomez-Mejia, L. R., Haynes, K. T., Nunez-Nickel, M., Jacobson, K. J. L., & Moyano-Fuentes, J. (2007). Socioemotional wealth and business risks in family-controlled firms: Evidence from Spanish olive oil mills. *Administrative Science Quarterly, 52*, 106–137.

Gordon, G., & Nicholson, N. (2008). *Family wars: Classic conflicts in family business and how to deal with them*. Kogan Page.

Harris-McKoy, D. (2016). Adolescent delinquency: Is too much or too little parental control a problem? *Journal of Child and Family Studies, 25*, 2079–2088.

Harrison, A., Summers, J., & Mennecke, B. (2018). The effects of the Dark Triad on unethical behavior. *Journal of Business Ethics, 153*, 53–77.

History.com Editors. (2011, July 20). *This day in history Dec 11, 2008, billionaire con man Bernie Madoff arrested*. https://www.history.com/this-day-in-history/billionaire-conman-bernard-madoff-arrested. Accessed October 20, 2023.

Hollander, B.S. (2002). Silver spoon syndrome. In C.E. Aronoff, J.H. Astrachan, & J.L. Ward (Eds.), *Family business sourcebook: a guide for families who own businesses and the professionals who serve them*, 3rd Edition (pp. 538–539). Family Enterprise Publishers.

Homans, G. C. (1958). Social behavior as exchange. *American Journal of Sociology, 63*(6), 597–606.

Huang, X., Chen, L., Xu, E., Lu, F., & Tam, K. C. (2020). Shadow of the prince: Parent-incumbents' coercive control over child-successors in family organizations. *Administrative Science Quarterly, 65*(3), 710–750.

Hudson, S., González-Gómez, H. V., & Claasen, C. (2019). Legitimacy, particularism and employee commitment and justice. *Journal of Business Ethics, 157*(3), 589–603.

Hunt, K. (2012, March 18). *Feuds threaten Asia's family businesses*. https://www.bbc.co.uk/news/business-17309144. Accessed October 15, 2023.

Jaskiewicz, P., Uhlenbruck, K., Balkin, D. B., & Reay, T. (2013). Is nepotism good or bad? Types of nepotism and implications for knowledge management. *Family Business Review, 26*(2), 121–139.
Jehn, K. A. (1995). A multimethod examination of the benefits and detriments of intragroup conflict. *Administrative Science Quarterly, 40*, 256–282.
Jehn, K. A., & Mannix, E. A. (2001). The dynamic nature of conflict: A longitudinal study of intragroup conflict and group performance. *Academy of Management Journal, 44*(2), 238–251.
Jeong, S. H., Kim, H., & Kim, H. (2022). Strategic nepotism in family director appointments: Evidence from family business groups in South Korea. *Academy of Management Journal, 65*(2), 656–682.
Kellermanns, F. W., & Eddleston, K. A. (2004). Feuding families: When conflict does a family firm good. *Entrepreneurship Theory and Practice, 28*(3), 209–228.
Kellermanns, F. W., & Eddleston, K. A. (2007). A family perspective on when conflict benefits family firm performance. *Journal of Business Research, 60*(10), 1048–1057.
Kellermanns, F. W., Eddleston, K. A., & Zellweger, T. M. (2012). Extending the socioemotional wealth perspective: A look at the dark side. *Entrepreneurship Theory and Practice, 36*, 1175–1182.
Kidwell, R. E., Cox, K. C., & Kloepfer, K. E. (2019). The diversity of deviance: How it can hurt (and help) families and family firms. In *The Palgrave handbook of heterogeneity among family firms* (pp. 643–672). Springer.
Kidwell, R. E., Eddleston, K. A., Kidwell, L. A., Cater, J. J., & Howard, E. (2023). *Dysfunctional behavior in family firms across individuals, families, firms, and environments* (Unpublished working paper).
Klotz, A. C., & Neubaum, D. O. (2016). Article commentary: Research on the dark side of personality traits in entrepreneurship: Observations from an organizational behavior perspective. *Entrepreneurship Theory and Practice, 40*(1), 7–17.
Kubíček, A., & Machek, O. (2020). Intrafamily conflicts in family businesses: A systematic review of the literature and agenda for future research. *Family Business Review, 33*(2), 194–227.
Laible, D. J., & Thompson, R. A. (2000). Mother-child discourse, attachment security, shared positive affect, and early conscience development. *Child Development, 71*, 1424–1440.
Liyanagamage, N., Fernando, M., & Gibbons, B. (2023). The emotional Machiavellian: Interactions between leaders and employees. *Journal of Business Ethics, 186*(3), 657–673.
Loignon, A. C., Kellermanns, F. W., Eddleston, K. A., & Kidwell, R. E. (2017). Bad blood in the boardroom: Antecedents and outcomes of conflict in the

family firm. In F. W. Kellermanns & F. Hoy (Eds.), *The Routledge companion to family business* (pp. 349–366). Routledge.

Lubatkin, M. H., Schulze, W. S., Ling, Y., & Dino, R. N. (2005). The effects of parental altruism on the governance of family-managed firms. *Journal of Organizational Behavior, 26*, 313–330.

Madden, T. M., Madden, L. T., Strickling, J. A., & Eddleston, K. A. (2017). Psychological contract and social exchange in family firms. *International Journal of Management and Enterprise Development, 16*(1–2), 109–127.

Madison, K., Daspit, J., Turner, K., & Kellermanns, F. (2018). Family firm human resource practices: Investigating the effects of professionalization and bifurcation bias on performance. *Journal of Business Research, 84*, 327–336.

McLarty, B. D., & Holt, D. T. (2019). A bright side to family firms: How socioemotional wealth importance affects dark traits–job performance relationships. *Family Business Review, 32*(4), 378–395.

McLarty, B. D., Skorodziyevskiy, V., & Muldoon, J. (2023). The Dark Triad's incremental influence on entrepreneurial intentions. *Journal of Small Business Management, 61*(4), 2097–2125.

Miller, D., Minichilli, A., & Corbetta, G. (2013). Is family leadership always beneficial? *Strategic Management Journal, 34*(5), 553–571.

Miller, D., Steier, L., & Le Breton-Miller, I. (2003). Lost in time: Intergenerational succession, change, and failure in family business. *Journal of Business Venturing, 18*(4), 513–531.

Paulhus, D. L. (2014). Toward a taxonomy of dark personalities. *Current Directions in Psychological Science, 23*(6), 421–426.

Paulhus, D. L., & Williams, K. M. (2002). The Dark Triad of personality: Narcissism, Machiavellianism, and psychopathy. *Journal of Research in Personality, 36*, 556–563.

Pillari, V. (1991). *Scapegoating in families: Intergenerational patterns of physical and emotional abuse*. Brunner/Mazel.

Poza, E. J. (2013). *Family business*. Cengage Learning.

Purkayastha, S., Veliyath, R., & George, R. (2022). Type I and type II agency conflicts in family firms: An empirical investigation. *Journal of Business Research, 153*, 285–299.

Richmond, M. K., & Stocker, C. M. (2008). Longitudinal associations between parents 'hostility and siblings' externalizing behavior in the context of marital discord. *Journal of Family Psychology, 22*(2), 231–240.

Rosecká, N., & Machek, O. (2022). Non-family members and conflict processes in family firms: A systematic review of literature. *Journal of Business Economics, 92*(2), 235–281.

Rousseau, D. M. (1989). Psychological and implied contracts in organizations. *Employee Responsibilities and Rights Journal, 2*, 121–139.

Qiu, H., & Freel, M. (2020). Managing family-related conflicts in family businesses: A review and research agenda. *Family Business Review, 33*(1), 90–113.

Samara, G., Jamali, D., & Parada, M. (2021). Antecedents and outcomes of bifurcated compensation in family firms: A multilevel view. *Human Resource Management Review, 31*(1). https://doi.org/10.1016/j.hrmr.2019.100728

Sanchez-Marin, G., Portillo-Navarro, M., & Clavel, J. (2016). The influence of family involvement on tax aggressiveness of family firms. *Journal of Family Business Management, 6*(2), 143–168.

Sanders, A., Szymanski, K., & Fiori, K. (2014). The family roles of siblings of people diagnosed with a mental disorder: Heroes and lost children. *International Journal of Psychology, 49*(4), 257–262.

Schulze, W., Lubatkin, M., Dino, R., & Buchholtz, A. (2001). Agency relationships in family firms: Theory and evidence. *Organization Science, 12*(2), 99–116.

Shanine, K. K., Madison, K., Combs, J. G., & Eddleston, K. A. (2023). Parenting the successor: It starts at home and leaves an enduring impact on the family business. *Entrepreneurship Theory and Practice, 47*(4), 1093–1131.

Spranger, J. L., Colarelli, S. M., Dimotakis, N., Jacob, A. C., & Arvey, R. D. (2012). Effects of kin density within family-owned businesses. *Organizational Behavior and Human Decision Processes, 119*(2), 151–162.

Swab, R. G., Sherlock, C., Markin, E., & Dibrell, C. (2020). "SEW" What do we know and where do we go? A review of socioemotional wealth and a way forward. *Family Business Review, 33*(4), 424–445.

Tang, Y., Ye, S., & Zhou, J. (2013). Political connections, legal environment, and corporate valuation in Chinese public family firms. *The Chinese Economy, 46*(6), 32–49.

Van den Berghe, L. A., & Carchon, S. (2003). Agency relations within the family business system: An exploratory approach. *Corporate Governance: An International Review, 11*(3), 171–179.

Ward, S. G., Envick, B. R., & Langford, M. (2007). On the theory of psychological contracts in family firms. *The Entrepreneurial Executive, 12*, 37–50.

Williams, K. M., Paulhus, D. L., & Hare, R. D. (2007). Capturing the four-factor structure of psychopathy in college students via self-report. *Journal of Personality Assessment, 88*(2), 205–219.

Yamanoi, J., & Asaba, S. (2018). The impact of family ownership on establishment and ownership modes in foreign direct investment: The moderating role of corruption in host countries. *Global Strategy Journal, 8*, 106–135.

Zagefka, H., Jones, J., Caglar, A., Girish, R., & Matos, C. (2021). Family roles, family dysfunction, and depressive symptoms. *The Family Journal, 29*(3), 346–353.

Zientara, P. (2017). Socioemotional wealth and corporate social responsibility: A critical analysis. *Journal of Business Ethics, 144*(1), 185–199.

CHAPTER 3

Negative Acts Within Family Firms

Abstract Various types of behaviors that can be deviant, dysfunctional, and damaging are reviewed, focusing on behaviors that are perpetrated by individuals and groups within the context of the family and the family firm. A brief discussion of assorted concept definitions and major theories used in the research of dysfunctional behaviors in family firms is followed by a review of specific behaviors that a perpetrator targets against individuals, the family, and the family firm. These negative acts include counterproductive work behavior, bullying, theft, withholding information, aggression, resistance to change, bias against non-family members, gender discrimination, and firm-level conflict. Although the heterogeneity of the behaviors in this category appears evident in terms of types and potential targets, the chapter discusses why there is relatively little research of these behaviors compared to other dysfunctional phenomena studied in the context of family firms.

Keywords Counterproductive behavior · Bifurcation bias · Gender discrimination · Firm-level conflict · Fredo effect · Agency theory · Stewardship theory · Family firms

R. E. Kidwell, *Dysfunction and Deviance Across Family Firms*, Palgrave Studies in Family Business Heterogeneity,
https://doi.org/10.1007/978-3-031-51816-4_3

> Once Bobby graduated from college, he joined the family's restaurant business managing the bar area despite his lack of experience. Although the head bartender was in charge of training him, she was not pleased that she would be sharing responsibilities with him. Bobby's father, Tony, noted that troubles with Bobby began almost immediately. He would consume cocktails while tending bar, give away excessive drinks to friends, and sexually harass waitresses waiting for their drink orders. He soon began stealing cash from the register, taking bottles of liquor home with him, and not showing up for work. Any other employee would be fired for such behavior, but Tony knew he couldn't turn away his own son. (Eddleston & Kidwell, 2012a)

The previous chapter focused on the heterogeneity of the antecedents of deviant and dysfunctional behavior emphasizing that some of the phenomena identified as precursors of dysfunction could also be contributors to family firms that function effectively. These included certain forms of conflict, nepotism, pursuit of socioemotional wealth, and early parental and family relationships. This chapter instead focuses on the different types of negative behaviors stemming from these potential antecedents that are perpetrated by individuals inside the firm and directed against the business or individuals and groups within it.

Negative workplace behavior at the individual level goes by many different names and definitions as indicated by the terms, classifications, and groupings of various constructs that were mentioned in Chapter 1 and have been used in the last quarter century of workplace research with relatively little specific focus on family firms until recently. The different terms and definitions used by researchers studying negative acts in the workplace are listed in Table 3.1.

Robinson (2008: 5) grouped deviance with counterproductive behavior in her review of related research on dysfunction in the workplace, stating that a "distinguishing feature of these behaviors is that although they are intentional behaviors that are potentially harmful (as opposed to accidents or poor performance, which are not intentional but potentially harmful), they are not necessarily intended by the actor to be harmful or destructive." This is a very valid point in a family business context.

As noted in the introductory chapter, dysfunction is used here as an umbrella term that encompasses willful negative acts in families and family firms that harm others whereas deviance refers to the breaking of family and/or family firm norms (Kidwell et al., 2023). Much of the scholarly research of negative workplace behaviors at the individual and

Table 3.1 Summary table of negative behaviors in the workplace

Term	*Definition*	*Source*	*Examples*
Dysfunctional behavior	Occurs when employees or groups of employees engage in activities that have negative consequences for an individual in an organization, a group of individuals, and/or the organization itself	Griffin et al. (1998) and Griffin and O'Leary-Kelly (2004)	There are two general types: violent and deviant (e.g., aggression, physical and verbal assault, terrorism) and non-violent dysfunctional (e.g., alcohol and drug use, revenge, absence, and theft)
Workplace deviance	"Voluntary behavior that violates significant organizational norms and, in doing so, threatens the well-being of the organization or its members, or both"	Bennett and Robinson (2000: 349)	Can be directed either at individuals, as reflected in behavior such as harassment, backstabbing, or physical aggression, or directed at the organization, as reflected in behavior such as theft, sabotage, or absenteeism
Counterproductive behavior	"Any intentional behavior on the part of an organization member viewed by the organization as contrary to its legitimate interests"	Sackett (2002: 5)	"Counterproductive behavior is considered an element of job performance. Examples can include theft, destruction of property, misuse of information, unsafe behavior, poor attendance, and poor work quality"

(continued)

Table 3.1 (continued)

Term	*Definition*	*Source*	*Examples*
Anti-social behavior	Behavior intended to bring harm to and/or does harm an organization, its employees, or the organization's stakeholders	Giacalone and Greenberg (1997)	It includes aggression, discrimination, theft, interpersonal violence, sabotage, harassment, lying, revenge, and whistleblowing. Anti-social behavior focuses primarily on personal and property interactions, and less so on production with the exception of sabotage
Organizational misbehavior	"Acts in the workplace that are done intentionally and constitute a violation of rules pertaining to such behavior"	Vardi and Weitz (2004: 3)	Intended to benefit an individual or an organization and intends to inflict damage. Examples include time wasting, absence, turnover, crime, and sexual harassment

dyadic levels has been informed by social exchange theory (e.g., Cropanzano et al., 2017). At the individual level, among these negative acts of particular interest to family firm researchers have been counterproductive behavior and other forms of dysfunction such as withholding information and effort, theft, and bullying. At the firm level, behaviors of interest include bias against non-family members, gender discrimination, and relationship conflict that has escalated to firm-level conflict, potentially affecting the entire organization. As noted, the common bond of all these behaviors involves willful acts that either violate organizational norms and/or have *potentially* negative consequences for the individual, the family, and the organization; some of the behaviors target other individuals while some target groups of individuals, and others target the family, the family business, and/or its leaders.

3.1 Theoretical Assumptions

In examining the nature of family firms, researchers often frame their studies using conflicting lenses in which to regard the firm, its leadership, and its functions (Eddleston et al., 2018). Either an agency (control) or a stewardship (collaboration) perspective determines how behavior of family members and governance of the firm is framed and explained (e.g., Chrisman et al., 2007; Davis et al., 2010; Le Breton-Miller & Miller, 2009; Madison et al., 2016) though these two viewpoints are contradictory. Agency theory follows the instrumental, business identity of the firm through its focus on self-serving behavior by family owners and managers, often an outcome of principal-principal agency conflict between the family and the firm in which the interests of the dominant family owners may differ from the interests of the non-family owners (Chrisman et al., 2007; Le Breton-Miller & Miller, 2009; Purkayastha et al., 2022; Schulze et al., 2001). In contrast, stewardship theory aligns with a firm's family identity by focusing on the values of the family and the value of a committed family-based workforce that functions together to achieve outcomes favorable to the long-term health of both the family and the firm (Davis et al., 2010; Eddleston & Kellermanns, 2007; Madison et al., 2016).

A focus on agency theory (to oversimplify—family connection bad) or stewardship theory (to oversimplify—family connection good) has guided research over a considerable period, but the actual effects of agency and stewardship on family firms are complex (e.g., Madison et al., 2016). The findings that family firms are generally good financial stewards (higher investments and higher risk tolerance) but poor organizational stewards (lower compensation and training, and higher turnover) (Neckebrouck et al., 2018) provide interesting insights into how, why, and what types of dysfunctional behavior might be expected to develop within many family firms. Differences in findings across family firms may be guided by the fact that more than a dozen theoretical perspectives have been employed by researchers doing work that focuses on what is described here as internally directed deviance and dysfunction (Kidwell et al., 2023). These negative acts are defined and discussed in the following subsections as individual behaviors and firm-level behaviors.

3.2 Individual Behaviors

> I have a very unique workplace bullying and mobbing case. My husband is the owner of the company, and his older brother is his partner. Many days the workers come close to my home. The worst one of the bullies is my husband's older brother. His bully attitude is quite contagious. His favorite tactic is telling blatant (often ugly) lies to our employees about me. At times he has even told our workers that I have made accusations against them that I have not made. This sort of lying gets our employees to join "brother bully" in his hatred toward me and then his mobbing team grows. There have been times that I cannot go outside my home without being subjected to all sorts of harassment. (Mari, The Circle—Mobbing within a Family Business, 2023)

As stated, management scholars have defined workplace deviance as employee behaviors that break significant organizational norms and threaten to harm the organization, members of the organization, or both (Robinson & Bennett, 1995). When family members develop a high level of entitlement coupled with a weak parent–child relationship, the conditions are ripe for a Fredo Effect in which a family member's incompetence, opportunistic behaviors, or ethically dubious actions can impede the firm's success (Eddleston & Kidwell, 2012b; Kidwell et al., 2012). The presence of a Fredo, named after the incompetent middle son from The Godfather books and films, can potentially result in damage to the firm and negative impact on employees, customers, and other stakeholders (Kidwell et al., 2013).

Fredo's incompetence and revenge against the family business are classic examples of an individual engaging in *counterproductive work behavior* (CWB), which is an intentional behavior by an individual that may harm the interests of an organization or its stakeholders (Zheng et al., 2017). Counterproductive work behavior has been copiously studied for years yet there is still little consensus on how the different acts that constitute a CWB relate to each other and how they should be categorized (Marcus et al., 2016). CWBs, which can be directed at the firm as well as at individuals such as supervisors and peers, have been examined at the interpersonal level in family firms, guided generally by social exchange and justice theories, but few studies have focused specifically on family firms (Berry et al., 2007, 2012; Mackey et al., 2021).

Those who have researched CWB in family firms have considered various negative workplace actions such as shirking rather than working (Chrisman et al., 2004) acting in secrecy and withholding information (Hadjielias et al., 2021), resistance to change (Chirico et al., 2018), bullying (Baillien et al., 2011), and theft of company property and/or time (O'Brien et al., 2018). The factors leading to these types of behaviors can be the result of individual personality issues such as Machiavellianism, narcissism, and psychopathy (Galvin et al., 2015; Montiel Mendez & Maciel, 2020), personal pride (Umans et al., 2020), family firm context, such as altruism, entitlement, and resultant feelings of unfairness and injustice (Cooper et al., 2013), and rebellion resulting from dysfunctional parent–child relationships (Eddleston & Kidwell, 2012b). Finally, non-family employees may resort to deviant behavior because of outgroup membership rather than ingroup status (Marler & Stanley, 2018), and their belief that the psychological contract has been violated.

Yet, there is a relative paucity of family firm research in this area considering that a great deal of inquiry has taken place on the general topics of bullying, withholding effort, employee theft, substance abuse, insubordination, and other behaviors that are considered deviant and destructive to individuals and organizations. Speculation on why this is the case is provided in the concluding comments of this chapter. Yet, the examples of Mari and others show there is no shortage of dysfunctional behavior that damages individuals involved in the family business.

3.3 Firm Level: Bifurcation Bias

Whereas negative acts committed by individuals and small groups within the family firm are potentially damaging to individuals, families, and the business, individual and group actions that are set at the firm level by the dominant coalition have the potential to do even greater harm. These behaviors may reflect both formal and informal policies, culture, norms, or values of the family and the firm that are enforced across the family firm. Two of these are bifurcation bias and gender discrimination, both involving negative treatment of others either as part of a formal or informal process, and both becoming of more interest to researchers in family firms.

Bifurcation bias is defined as the unequal treatment of family and non-family members in a family firm (Verbeke & Kano, 2012). Various studies have addressed the topic in recent years both theoretically and empirically.

Several existing theoretical perspectives have been applied to the study of unequal treatment of non-family members. These viewpoints include SEW/behavioral agency theory (Laffranchini et al., 2022), agency theory (Madison et al., 2018), organizational justice (Waterwall & Alipour, 2021), circumplex theory (Daspit et al., 2018), and SEW/cultural dimensions/equity (Samara et al., 2021). Efforts toward developing a theory of bifurcation bias in family firms have taken HRM (Jennings et al., 2018) and social identity (Kim & Marler, 2020) perspectives.

Whereas a key antecedent of bias against non-family members in hiring and promotion would seem to relate to the level of nepotism practiced in the family business, researchers have considered how the level of professionalization of a family firm's human resource function tempers unequal treatment of non-family employees (Daspit et al., 2018; Jennings et al., 2018) and how that treatment can impact firm performance (Madison et al., 2018). To explain differences across firms, other researchers identified blood relatedness as an important determinant of bias against non-family members, influenced by societal factors such as collectivism and individual factors including familial proximity and familial tenure (Kim & Marler, 2020). Samara and colleagues (2021) proposed that family firms in collectivist cultures engage in bifurcation bias regarding compensation favoring family members, guided by a moral obligation to satisfy the family's financial well-being. In individualist cultures, the authors argued that if preference occurs it is more likely in favor of non-family employees.

The heterogeneity of the phenomenon is further indicated by research findings that studied its impact on performance. For example, bifurcation bias is seen as an obstacle to family firms' successful internationalization because it can negatively influence their decisions on which international markets to pursue and when to enter them (Kano & Verbeke, 2018). It can also impact non-family employees' organizational identification, which may influence non-family employees' willingness to engage in organizational citizenship behaviors, even when the firm is facing challenging times (Medina-Craven et al., 2021). In addition, bifurcation bias may obstruct the transition between entrepreneurial intention and action in family firms (Schepers et al., 2021). However, Waterwall and Alipour (2021) point out that organizational justice theory explains how non-family members' perceptions of their treatment when compared to family members may shape their behavioral intentions differently in some family firms. They concluded that any unequal treatment of non-family employees may not be as harmful to family firms as has been suggested. Thus, the research indicates that internal bias against non-family members has the potential for diverse effects on family firms depending on a variety of factors about the family, the firm, and the environment in which it operates.

3.4 Firm Level: Gender Discrimination

Women's involvement in family firms has been studied for many years but has attracted more interest recently with a focus on women taking greater leadership roles in moving the family business forward (Boukhabza & Ouhadi, 2023; Campopiano et al., 2017; Maseda et al., 2022). These recent literature reviews found a great deal of focus on women's entrepreneurial entry to the family firm, generational succession, career dynamics, and the woman's presence in the firm. The reviews discussed women's invisibility factor and unequal treatment compared to male siblings and other men in hindering progress into the firm and rising to lead it. Clearly, women's struggle in entering and establishing themselves in family firms has long been a topic of research interest, reformulated in this chapter as potential gender discrimination. Even though gender discrimination may not be seen as deviant in the past as it conformed to a prevailing norm, it has the potential to be dysfunctional to the firm—and the family.

Early practitioner-oriented family business studies described women as often invisible in the firm (Dumas, 1989), and their qualifications were not recognized either inside or outside of the family firm (Hollander & Bukowitz, 1990) even though they served as emotional leaders of families and family firms. For example, women kept communication lines open among family members (Salganicoff, 1990), which potentially encouraged conflicts between parents and siblings to be resolved. Although successful female leadership and ownership of family firms has been documented (Cadieux et al., 2002), more recently, researchers have focused on the occurrence and impact of gender discrimination within firms as societal norms have shifted.

Gender norms continue to have a strong impact on females not seeking ascendency to leadership in family firms. Males are still chosen most often as successors (in more than 75% of the cases), and a preference for male successors can limit the available candidates for family firms (Ahrens et al., 2015). Daughters may not even consider succession to firm leadership until they are motivated to do so by a critical event (Overbeke et al., 2013) such as a death or incapacitation of senior leaders. However, trends indicate that women are becoming members of team leadership structures (Cater et al., 2016). Family businesses trail non-family firms in gender representation, suggesting family firms do not fully realize the potential advantages of female leadership. However, family firms are more successful in closing gender compensation gaps in their firms' top management teams (Jain et al., 2021).

Whereas progress for women has been made regarding ascendency to family firm leadership (Moran, 2015), several factors continue to stymie females from leadership positions in family businesses; some of these relate to cultural norms as well as the culture and structure of many family firms (Boukhabza & Ouhadi, 2023.). For example, financial mechanisms protecting the family from traditional corporate governance systems allow dominant shareholders to neutralize the potential advantages of female leadership in family firms and gain benefits at others' expense (Chadwick & Dawson, 2018). Even if a family firm has established a culture of fairness and respect, it may lack a formal code of ethics that would guard against such dysfunctional behaviors as gender discrimination (Fischer & Friedman, 2021).

3.5 Firm Level: Conflict

> My oldest sister has split the whole family apart. I don't talk with my sisters. ... I don't know if it was greed, or if this guy (brother-in-law) wanted control. To me, it was a conspiracy theory or something. The girls saw this money if you get rid of three or four of the boys. ... Unaware to me, there was a Power of Attorney. The Power of Attorney was brought up and the sisters have control. ... When Momma passes away, there will be World War III . ... It is a bloodbath with family business. (Second-generation family firm member, quoted in Cater et al., 2016: 19–20)

Family firms are well-known for complex levels of conflict. Because family members' lives often are linked together in the family business, this limits individual career paths and success, often resulting in feuds that transcend interpersonal, relationship-oriented conflict between individuals (Stamm, 2016). Firm-level conflict occurs when any of the three types of conflict (task, process, relationship) escalate to produce discord among family firm leadership. At this stage, the conflict can still be mitigated and potentially turned into a positive outcome depending on effective management of the conflict. Otherwise, the acts and conditions that result in conflict at the organizational level can hurt a family business's succession process, firm performance, business family relations, and governance of the firm.

When a dispute leads family members to take sides (Minichilli et al., 2010) or when there is complexity of ownership across multiple generations (Sacristan-Navarro & Cabeza-Garcia, 2019), damaging firm-level conflict can develop, hurting the company's financial performance. Many firm-level conflicts that can potentially impact family firm outcomes involve governance issues such as active and passive owner/agency disputes (Blanco-Mazagatos et al., 2016), clashes regarding owner-manager governance (Purkayastha et al., 2019, 2022), and the effects of family dynamics and altruism on agency conflicts (Schulze et al., 2001).

Multiple studies of family conflict address the issue of divorce in family firms. Researchers found that high levels of debt and high sales revenues in family firms were stressors that significantly increased divorce rates (Sanchez-Ruiz et al., 2018). Haag and Sund (2016) observed that family law is not well suited for family businesses because the firm is considered merely an asset that needs to divided, leaving firm management issues poorly addressed, and this often results in even greater dysfunctional firm-level conflict. Relationship conflicts among couples, siblings, cousins, in-laws, and others—or between generations—also may escalate to firm-level conflicts and threaten the future of the business (Jayantilal et al., 2016).

However, studies regarding these firm-level conflicts illustrate the diversity of family firms. Minichilli and colleagues (2010) argued for a bright side as well as a dark side of family involvement in concluding that family firm factions may harm business performance even if the CEO is a family member. In addition, family firm owners may differ in their strategic preferences and goals, and these differences can lead to damaging conflict over the owners' growth expectations for the firm (Calabro et al., 2017). Yet, other studies found that firm-level conflict need not have negative results if mechanisms to contain its dysfunctional effects are employed. For example, balancing family ownership with non-family management can effectively address most principal-agent conflicts and positively affect principal-principal conflicts (Purkayastha et al., 2019,

2022). In addition, the increased conflict and power struggles that result from multiple generations of ownership with different interests could be alleviated with governance mechanisms such as a family council and a family constitution—or, if necessary, established procedures for liquidation of family members' ownership interests (Sacristan-Navarro & Cabeza-Garcia, 2019).

3.6 Concluding Comments

An emphasis in this chapter has been on negative behaviors directed internally that have the capacity to hurt others as well as the firm. Perpetrators of dysfunction may engage in aggressive acts such as harassment and bullying of co-workers, both family members and non-family members, or they may be passive and withhold effort toward the completion of tasks based on their status as family members, or they may exact reprisal against perceived unfairness. They may act in ways that harm the firm through theft or badmouthing or may have good intentions in their actions yet their lack of competence results in disaster. They may discriminate against women or non-family members but do so because they believe they are acting in accordance with company traditions and/or policies.

However, as noted in Chapter 2, the antecedents of deviance and dysfunction can result in noble behaviors that lead to positive effects. Conflict, if properly managed, can result in better decision making and more inclusive points of view. The firm context can produce merit-based reward systems that incentivize and encourage family and non-family alike to pursue high levels of performance and innovative behaviors. Nepotism policies can cement behaviors reflecting dedication and loyalty to the firm by family members who will evolve into effective leaders. Early family relationships can produce heroes and ingroup members who will do good work in the family business. These antecedents can also deviate from family firm norms in a positive way leading to such behaviors as innovation in a stagnant family firm. Thus, the heterogeneity of the behaviors that stem from what are first identified as negative antecedents is clear.

Despite recent interest in counterproductive work behavior and other forms of general dysfunction in family firms (Baillien et al., 2011; Marler & Stanley, 2018; O'Brien et al., 2018), relatively few empirical studies have been published. A great deal of research based on the constructs shown in Table 3.1 has been done at the individual level regarding negative behaviors in all types of organizations. This may be one reason why there has been relatively little research that considers family business. However, family businesses and families have a uniqueness that should be a focus of future research. Relationships among employees, owners, and managers distinguish family firms from non-family firms and from one another as do the nuances of family relationships that can impact individual dysfunction at work. Concepts unique to the family firm such as socioemotional wealth, familiness, and parent–child relationships could also be brought into play to a greater extent. Thus, increased focus on attitudes and emotions, the firm context and the family context combined with personality traits and their relationship to dysfunctional behavior is an important area for family firm research (e.g., Barnett & Kellermanns, 2006) that could help uncover the impact of the family on an individual's engagement in dysfunctional behavior (Eddleston & Kidwell, 2012b; McLarty & Holt, 2019).

Within family firms, dysfunctional behaviors are important, but they do not often involve publicized crimes and are very difficult for family members to discuss candidly with outsiders, advisors as well as researchers, because they involve close relationships with people about whom they care. For example, one family member does not want to discuss another family member stealing from the company or underperforming as it reflects poorly on the family as well as the business. Thus, it was surprising to find that as many as 30% of family firm survey respondents *admitted* they had a Fredo, i.e., a family member who impeded the activities of their family firms (Kidwell et al., 2012).

Researchers were taken aback that so many respondents would reveal this to strangers even though it was suspected that the actual percentage was probably much higher. These acts—within the firm, carried out by individual rank-and-file family Fredos, by non-family members, or by members of the dominant coalition—hurt the family and the firm. But these behaviors lend themselves to more elusive and rich qualitative research approaches than more available and less-rich secondary and archival data sources, which are often used for research into other types of dysfunctions. The in-firm escapades are also not big newsmakers unlike the fraud and bribery scandals described in the next chapter.

References

Ahrens, J. P., Landmann, A., & Woywode, M. (2015). Gender preferences in the CEO successions of family firms: Family characteristics and human capital of the successor. *Journal of Family Business Strategy, 6*(2), 86–103.

Baillien, E., Neyens, I., & De Witte, H. (2011). Organizational correlates of workplace bullying in small-and medium-sized enterprises. *International Small Business Journal, 29*(6), 610–625.

Barnett, T., & Kellermanns, F. W. (2006). Are we family and are we treated as family? Nonfamily employees' perceptions of justice in the family firm. *Entrepreneurship Theory and Practice, 30*(6), 837–854.

Bennett, R. J., & Robinson, S. L. (2000). Development of a measure of workplace deviance. *Journal of Applied Psychology, 85*(3), 349–360.

Berry, C. M., Carpenter, N. C., & Barratt, C. L. (2012). Do other-reports of counterproductive work behavior provide an incremental contribution over self-reports? A meta-analytic comparison. *Journal of Applied Psychology, 97*, 613–636.

Berry, C. M., Ones, D. S., & Sackett, P. R. (2007). Interpersonal deviance, organizational deviance, and their common correlates: A review and meta-analysis. *Journal of Applied Psychology, 92*, 410–424.

Blanco-Mazagatos, V., Quevedo-Puente, E., & Delgado-Garcia, J. (2016). How agency conflict, between family managers and family owners affects performance in wholly family-owned firms: A generational perspective. *Journal of Family Business Strategy, 7*, 167–177.

Boukhabza, S., Ouhadi, S. (2023). Women in family business succession: a systematic literature review and future research agenda. *Management Review Quarterly*, https://doi.org/10.1007/s11301-023-00366-0

Cadieux, L., Lorrain, J., & Hugron, P. (2002). Succession in women-owned family businesses: A case study. *Family Business Review, 15*(1), 17–30.

Calabro, A., Campopiano, G., & Basco, R. (2017). Principal-principal conflicts and family firm growth: The moderating role of business family identity. *Journal of Family Business Management, 7*(3), 291–308.

Campopiano, G., De Massis, A., Rinaldi, F. R., & Sciascia, S. (2017). Women's involvement in family firms: Progress and challenges for future research. *Journal of Family Business Strategy, 8*(4), 200–212.

Cater, J. J., III., Kidwell, R. E., & Camp, K. M. (2016). Successor team dynamics in family firms. *Family Business Review, 29*(3), 301–326.

Chadwick, I. C., & Dawson, A. (2018). Women leaders and firm performance in family businesses: An examination of financial and nonfinancial outcomes. *Journal of Family Business Strategy, 9*(4), 238–249.

Chirico, F., Salvato, C., Byrne, B., Akhter, N., & Arriaga Múzquiz, J. (2018). Commitment escalation to a failing family business. *Journal of Small Business Management, 56*(3), 494–512.

Chrisman, J. J., Chua, J. H., Kellermanns, F. W., & Chang, E. P. (2007). Are family managers agents or stewards? An exploratory study in privately held family firms. *Journal of Business Research, 60*(10), 1030–1038.

Chrisman, J. J., Chua, J. H., & Litz, R. A. (2004). Comparing the agency costs of family and non-family firms: Conceptual issues and exploratory evidence. *Entrepreneurship Theory and Practice, 28*, 335–354.

Cooper, J. T., Kidwell, R. E., & Eddleston, K. A. (2013). Boss and parent, employee and child: Work-family roles and deviant behavior in the family firm. *Family Relations, 62*(3), 457–471.

Cropanzano, R., Anthony, E. L., Daniels, S. R., & Hall, A. V. (2017). Social exchange theory: A critical review with theoretical remedies. *Academy of Management Annals, 11*(1), 479–516.

Daspit, J., Madison, K., Barnett, T., & Long, R. (2018). The emergence of bifurcation bias from unbalanced families: Examining HR practices in the family firm using circumplex theory. *Human Resource Management Review, 28*(1), 18–32.

Davis, J. H., Allen, M. R., & Hayes, H. D. (2010). Is blood thicker than water? A study of stewardship perceptions in family business. *Entrepreneurship Theory and Practice, 34*(6), 1093–1116.

Dumas, C. (1989). Understanding the father-daughter and the father-son dyads in family-owned businesses. *Family Business Review, 2*, 31–47.

Eddleston, K. A., & Kellermanns, F. W. (2007). Destructive and productive family relationships: A stewardship theory perspective. *Journal of Business Venturing, 22*(4), 545–565.

Eddleston, K. A., Kellermanns, F. W., & Kidwell, R. E. (2018). Managing family members: How monitoring and collaboration affect extra-role behavior in family firms. *Human Resource Management, 57*(5), 957–977.

Eddleston, K. A., & Kidwell, R. E. (2012a). The bad seed's poisonous harvest: How offspring sow and reap deviant and dysfunctional behavior in the family business. In A. Carsrud & M. Brännback (Eds.), *Understanding family businesses: Undiscovered approaches, unique perspectives and neglected topics* (pp. 95–114). Springer.

Eddleston, K. A., & Kidwell, R. E. (2012b). Parent-child relationships: Planting the seeds of deviant behavior in the family firm. *Entrepreneurship Theory & Practice, 36*(2), 369–386.

Fischer, D., & Friedman, H. (2021). Family business in the #MeToo era: Lessons from Ruth on tone at the top. *Humanistic Management Journal, 6*, 37–55.

Galvin, B. M., Lange, D., & Ashforth, B. E. (2015). Narcissistic organizational identification: Seeing oneself as central to the organization's identity. *Academy of Management Review, 40*(2), 163–181.

Griffin, R. W., & O'Leary-Kelly, A. (2004). *The dark side of organizational behavior*. Wiley.

Griffin, R. W., O'Leary-Kelly, A., & Collins, J. M. (1998). *Dysfunctional behavior in organizations: Violent and deviant behavior*. Monographs in Organizational Behavior and Industrial Relations (Vol. 23). JAI Press.

Giacalone, R. A., & Greenberg, J. (Eds.). (1997). *Antisocial behavior in organizations*. Thousand Oaks, CA: Sage.

Haag, K., & Sund, L. G. (2016). Divorce in the family business: Unfolding the legal problems by learning from practice. *Journal of Family Business Management, 6*(1), 81–96.

Hadjielias, E., Christofi, M., & Tarba, S. (2021). Knowledge hiding and knowledge sharing in small family farms: A stewardship view. *Journal of Business Research, 137*, 279–292.

Hollander, B. S., & Bukowitz, W. R. (1990). Women, family culture and family business. *Family Business Review, 3*, 139–151.

Jain, S. S., Fernando, G. D., Tripathy, A., & Bhatia, S. (2021). Closing the gender gap in top management teams: An examination of diversity and compensation parity in family and non-family firms. *Journal of Family Business Strategy, 12*(4). https://doi.org/10.1016/j.jfbs.2020.100388

Jayantilal, S., Jorge, S. F., & Palacios, T. M. B. (2016). Effects of sibling competition on family firm succession: A game theory approach. *Journal of Family Business Strategy, 7*(4), 260–268.

Jennings, J., Dempsey, D., & James, A. (2018). Bifurcated HR practices in family firms: Insights from the normative-adaptive approach to stepfamilies. *Human Resource Management Review, 28*(1), 68–82.

Kano, L., & Verbeke, A. (2018). Family firm internationalization: Heritage assets and the impact of bifurcation bias. *Global Strategy Journal, 8*(1), 158–183.

Kidwell, R. E., Eddleston, K. A., Cater, J. J., & Kellermanns, F. W. (2013). How one bad family member can undermine a family firm: Preventing the Fredo effect. *Business Horizons, 56*(1), 5–12.

Kidwell, R. E., Eddleston, K. A., Kidwell, L. A., Cater, J. J., & Howard, E. (2023). *Dysfunctional behavior in family firms across individuals, families, firms, and environments* (Unpublished working paper).

Kidwell, R. E., Kellermanns, F. W., & Eddleston, K. A. (2012). Harmony, justice, confusion and conflict in the family firm: Implications for ethical climate and the "Fredo effect." *Journal of Business Ethics, 106*, 503–517.

Kim, T., & Marler, L. (2020). Are non-blood related "family" members treated differently? Determinants of bifurcation bias among family members in the family firm. *Journal of Family Business Management, 12*(1), 136–151.

Laffranchini, G., Hadjimarcou, J., & Kim, S. (2022). The first turnaround response of family firms in a crisis situation. *Journal of Family Business Strategy, 13*(1). https://doi.org/10.1016/j.jfbs.2021.100434

Le Breton-Miller, I., & Miller, D. (2009). Agency vs. stewardship in public family firms: A social embeddedness reconciliation. *Entrepreneurship Theory and Practice, 33*(6), 1169–1191.

Mackey, J. D., McAllister, C. P., Ellen, B. P., III., & Carson, J. E. (2021). A meta-analysis of interpersonal and organizational workplace deviance research. *Journal of Management, 47*, 597–622.

Madison, K., Daspit, J., Turner, K., & Kellermanns, F. (2018). Family firm human resource practices: Investigating the effects of professionalization and bifurcation bias on performance. *Journal of Business Research, 84*, 327–336.

Madison, K., Holt, D. T., Kellermanns, F. W., & Ranft, A. L. (2016). Viewing family firm behavior and governance through the lens of agency and stewardship theories. *Family Business Review, 29*(1), 65–93.

Marcus, B., Taylor, O. A., Hastings, S. E., Sturm, A., & Weigelt, O. (2016). The structure of counterproductive work behavior: A review, a structural meta-analysis, and a primary study. *Journal of Management, 42*(1), 203–233.

Mari. (2023). *The circle—Mobbing within a family business*. https://www.overcomebullying.org/the-circle-mobbing-within-a-family-business.html. Accessed October 8, 2023.

Marler, L. E., & Stanley, L. J. (2018). Commentary: Who are your friends? The influence of identification and family in-group and out-group friendships on nonfamily employee OCB and deviance. *Entrepreneurship Theory and Practice, 42*(2), 310–316.

Maseda, A., Iturralde, T., Cooper, S., & Aparicio, G. (2022). Mapping women's involvement in family firms: A review based on bibliographic coupling analysis. *International Journal of Management Reviews, 24*(2), 279–305.

McLarty, B. D., & Holt, D. T. (2019). A bright side to family firms: How socioemotional wealth importance affects dark traits–job performance relationships. *Family Business Review, 32*(4), 378–395.

Medina-Craven, M. N., Cooper, D., Penney, C., & Caldas, M. P. (2021). Family firm employees: Identification, stewardship practices and citizenship behaviors. *Journal of Family Business Management, 11*(4), 538–554.

Minichilli, A., Corbetta, G., & MacMillan, I. C. (2010). Top management teams in family-controlled companies: 'Familiness,' 'faultlines,' and their impact on financial performance. *Journal of Management Studies, 47*(2), 205–222.

Montiel Mendez, O. J., & Maciel, A. S. (2020). Dark side of the family business: An exploratory perspective. *Journal of Family Business Management, 11*(4), 386–401.

Moran, G. (2015). *Exclusive: This is the type of business most likely to promote women leaders*. https://fortune.com/2015/06/18/family-business-women-leaders. Accessed October 10, 2023.

Neckebrouck, J., Schulze, W., & Zellweger, T. (2018). Are family firms good employers? *Academy of Management Journal, 61*(2), 553–585.

O'Brien, K. E., Minjock, R. M., Colarelli, S. M., & Yang, C. (2018). Kinship ties and employee theft perceptions in family-owned businesses. *European Management Journal, 36*(3), 421–430.

Overbeke, K. K., Bilimoria, D., & Perelli, S. (2013). The dearth of daughter successors in family businesses: Gendered norms, blindness to possibility, and invisibility. *Journal of Family Business Strategy, 4*(3), 201–212.

Purkayastha, S., Veliyath, R., & George, R. (2019). The roles of family ownership and family management in the governance of agency conflicts. *Journal of Business Research, 98*, 50–64.

Purkayastha, S., Veliyath, R., & George, R. (2022). Type I and type II agency conflicts in family firms: An empirical investigation. *Journal of Business Research, 153*, 285–299.

Robinson, S. L. (2008). Dysfunctional workplace behavior. In J. Barling & C. L. Cooper (Eds.), *The Sage handbook of organizational behavior* (Vol. 1, pp. 141–159). Sage.

Robinson, S. L., & Bennett, R. J. (1995). A typology of deviant workplace behaviors: A multidimensional scaling study. *Academy of Management Journal, 38*(2), 555–572.

Sackett, P. R. (2002). The structure of counterproductive work behaviors: Dimensionality and relationships with facets of job performance. *International Journal of Selection and Assessment, 10*, 5–11.

Sacristan-Navarro, M., & Cabeza-Garcia, L. (2019). When family firm corporate governance fails: The case of E1 Corte Ingles. *Journal of Family Business Management, 10*(2), 97–115.

Salganicoff, M. (1990). Women in family businesses: Challenges and opportunities. *Family Business Review, 3*(2), 125–137.

Samara, G., Jamali, D., & Parada, M. (2021). Antecedents and outcomes of bifurcated compensation in family firms: A multilevel view. *Human Resource Management Review, 31*(1). https://doi.org/10.1016/j.hrmr.2019.100728

Sanchez-Ruiz, P., Maldonado-Bautista, I., & Rutherford, M. (2018). Business stressors, family-business identity, and divorce in family business: A vulnerability-stress-adaptation (VSA) model. *Journal of Family Business Strategy, 9*(3), 167–179.

Schepers, J., Voordeckers, W., Steijvers, T., & Laveren, E. (2021). Entrepreneurial intention-action gap in family firms: Bifurcation bias and the board of directors as an economizing mechanism. *Eurasian Business Review, 11*(3), 451–475.

Schulze, W., Lubatkin, M., Dino, R., & Buchholtz, A. (2001). Agency relationships in family firms: Theory and evidence. *Organization Science, 12*(2), 99–116.

Stamm, I. K. (2016). Coordination tasks and negotiation modes of linked lives in entrepreneurial families. *Journal of Marriage and Family, 78*(4), 939–956.

Umans, I., Lybaert, N., Steijvers, T., & Voordeckers, W. (2020). Succession planning in family firms: Family governance practices, board of directors, and emotions. *Small Business Economics, 54*(1), 189–207.
Vardi, Y., & Weitz, E. (2004). *Misbehavior in organizations: Theory, research, and management*. Lawrence Erlbaum Associates.
Verbeke, A., & Kano, L. (2012). The transaction cost economics theory of the family firm: Family-based human asset specificity and the bifurcation bias. *Entrepreneurship Theory and Practice, 36*, 1183–1205.
Waterwall, B., & Alipour, K. (2021). Nonfamily employees' perceptions of treatment in family businesses: Implications for organizational attraction, job pursuit intentions, work attitudes, and turnover intentions. *Journal of Family Business Strategy, 12*(3). https://doi.org/10.1016/j.jfbs.2020.100387
Zheng, W., Wu, Y. C. J., Chen, X., & Lin, S. J. (2017). Why do employees have counterproductive work behavior? The role of founder's Machiavellianism and the corporate culture in China. *Management Decision, 55*(3), 563–578.

CHAPTER 4

Damaging Behavior Directed Outside the Family Firm

Abstract The focus of the chapter is on negative behaviors committed by family firm leaders and members and directed outside the firm. These negative acts target and impact the family business's external stakeholders and the business itself. They include fraud, financial misconduct, bribery/corruption, tax avoidance, tax evasion, and corporate social irresponsibility including negative environmental performance. Researchers across such disciplines as management, accounting, economics, and finance, working in the areas of financial misconduct, earnings management, tax avoidance/evasion, and fraud focus on behaviors by family firms that are often unethical or illegal yet in some cases are regarded as responsible and legal business practices, e.g., tax avoidance.

Keywords Fraud · Financial misconduct · Earnings management · Bribery · Corruption · Corporate social irresponsibility · Environmental performance · White-collar crime · Family firms

The heterogeneity of family firm behaviors and their degrees of dysfunction are apparent when considering negative acts that originate within the family firm and affect stakeholders who largely reside outside it. Whereas family members and their firms can be damaged when their leaders

R. E. Kidwell, *Dysfunction and Deviance Across Family Firms*, Palgrave Studies in Family Business Heterogeneity,
https://doi.org/10.1007/978-3-031-51816-4_4

and members perpetrate behaviors such as fraud, financial misconduct, bribery, corruption, corporate social irresponsibility, negative environmental performance, and tax aggressiveness, the targets in these cases are external to the family business. In this chapter, several different types of dysfunctional and deviant behaviors are identified and discussed in terms of their origin within the family firm, the intentions of the perpetrators of these behaviors, the nature of the victims of the behavior, and the potential for varying outcomes. In brief, such acts may hurt other interested parties but often benefit the family firm by cutting its costs, allowing it to pay less in taxes, and garnering it an unfair advantage over competitors (Kidwell et al., 2023). The differential impact of these behaviors on external stakeholders will be elaborated upon in the next chapter.

Much of the research into these types of negative acts compares their occurrence and effects in family versus non-family firms; but studies are increasingly focused on differences in these behaviors across family firms. Such differences include the legal and ethical nature of some behaviors versus others. Indeed, the question arises as to whether some of the acts that will be discussed such as earnings management and tax avoidance should even be considered dysfunctional or deviant. Dysfunctional and deviant behavior directed outside the family business can be regarded in two ways: acts that are motivated because of conditions and demands in the external environment and acts that affect the external environment. In this chapter, we provide an overview of the behaviors themselves, demonstrating differences in definitions as well as differences in how they are regarded.

The recent example of a parking service at a British airport illustrates a series of externally directed bad behaviors that financially benefited a family firm but had dysfunctional consequences for its stakeholders. Although the service, operated by a family firm near Manchester Airport, boasted that it offered safe and secure parking, customers found the opposite to be the case. The firm, run under several different names by Mohammed Isaq and his family from their home near the airport, promised customer satisfaction, but their services were a disaster. Hundreds of people returned from their vacations to find their vehicles badly damaged while others found drugs and weapons in their cars. And some passengers came home from vacation to find their cars had completely disappeared (Walker, 2023). The family firm may have gained financially in the short term, but the business was exposed, and family members faced criminal charges.

4.1 Fraud

Phenomena that relate to firm-level financial dysfunction include financial fraud, which involves illegality, and financial misconduct, which may or may not be illegal. Research into fraud is often based on agency theory, as information asymmetry between different types of owners allows family members to benefit at the expense of non-family investors (Anderson et al., 2017; Ghafoor et al., 2019a, 2019b). Family firm fraud has also been explained by the fraud triangle (Ghafoor et al., 2019a), in which perpetrators commit fraud based on pressure, opportunity, and a way to rationalize their actions (Cressey, 1953). Alternatively, Gottschalk and Asting (2019) considered family and non-family temptations to commit fraud under the theory of convenience. The theory of convenience proposes that a person's convenience orientation determines whether that individual, otherwise respected in his or her profession, will commit white-collar crime such as fraud based on the level of financial motives and the greed benefiting the individual or the organization, an opportunity to commit and conceal the crime, and a personal willingness to engage in deviant behavior (Gottschalk, 2020).

Other researchers have employed different conceptual approaches. For example, Ding and Wu (2014) examined the risk of embezzlement, theft, and fraud in different life stages of the firm as signaling the importance of socioemotional wealth, the pursuit of the family's non-economic goals beyond financial motivations. Krishnan and Peytcheva (2019) used the competing theories of entrenchment and alignment to find that auditors perceive that fraud risk is higher in family firms. Finally, Nilakantan and colleagues (2021) examined fraud in microloans using resource dependence theory, which considers the impact of relevant resources and the ability to access them.

Empirical findings of these fraud studies indicate that family firms are disproportionately subject to enforcement actions by stock market regulators compared to non-family firms (Anderson et al., 2017; Ghafoor et al., 2019a). Enforcement actions generally follow investigations into suspected fraud in publicly traded companies and do not necessarily result in criminal prosecution. But they can have a significant impact on a family firm's ability to get outside funding (Ghafoor et al., 2019b). Penalties can also include the removal of firm directors or executives, endangering the family's management. Ghafoor et al. (2019a) framed their work using elements of the fraud triangle, where financial difficulties may lead family members to take advantage of their unique access to information, as well as the potential to manipulate it, for personal gain, rationalizing that their fraudulent behavior is for the sake of the family. However, they found that the presence of institutional investors, an independent board, an effective audit committee, and the presence of a female on the board all provided active monitoring and increased oversight, thus lowering opportunity and reducing fraud occurrence. They concluded that disproportionate enforcement against family firms in Malaysia, the focus of the study, resulted from increased scrutiny by regulators, rather than a higher incidence of fraud. However, it would be difficult to arrive at the same conclusion in the United States considering Anderson et al.'s (2017) finding that more than 70 percent of SEC enforcement actions over a 25-year period involved family firms. The level of enforcement actions in the United States dropped dramatically after the departure of the founder, however, leading Anderson et al. (2017) to conclude that founders commit more fraud due to inexperience and arrogance, rather than some darker force.

Ding and Wu (2014) looked at smaller family firms, relying on self-reports of whether firms had committed misconduct in the past, defining misconduct as theft, embezzlement, or fraud. They found that, among older firms, family firms are less likely than non-family firms to commit financial misconduct. However, that reduced likelihood only develops when the owners are older and likely to be considering their legacy. When the owner or the firm is younger, there is no difference between family and non-family firms in the prevalence of financial misconduct.

Another signal of the perception of fraud risk among family firms is how willing auditors are to take on new family firm clients. Krishnan and Peytcheva (2019) found that auditors assess the risk of fraud as higher for family firms, perceiving more severe agency conflicts to be present in family firms than in non-family firms, and were therefore less likely to make client acceptance recommendations for family firms. Their findings were consistent with entrenchment theory, which sees fraud to be more likely in family firms because the dominant ownership of the family creates incentives for family members to take wealth from minority shareholders, and inconsistent with attachment theory, which argues that fraud is less likely in family firms due to their concentration of ownership and control. However, the strength of the firm's audit committee moderates the family firm effect, as it reduces the likelihood of fraud.

In the microfinance realm, unethical behavior may be more related to violations of the funding contract and resulting harm to household welfare. In India, microloans are generally targeted at women who both own and operate small businesses. However, when men in the household take over operations, it both violates the contract and reduces household wealth, because men are more likely to spend for immediate gain at the expense of the household (Nilakantan et al., 2021).

4.2 Financial Misconduct

Financial misconduct is an area where a diversity of opinion exists as to whether all forms of it should be classified as illegal or even unethical, thus calling into question the level of dysfunction it represents. Examples of this behavior include earnings management, earnings manipulation, insider trading, and activities that potentially damage or threaten the firm's actual financial performance.

A heterogeneity of viewpoints is evident when earnings management is contrasted with earnings manipulation. Earnings management is defined by Ning (2009:36) as "exercising the discretion accorded by accounting standards and corporate laws, and/or structuring activities in such a way that expected firm value is not affected negatively." On the other hand, earnings manipulation involves actions taken by management to bring about a desired level of reported earnings by artificially inflating revenue and deflating expenses by deferring maintenance, delaying spending to the next reporting period, or incentivizing customers to buy products earlier than they would normally order them (Ning (2009). Earnings management and manipulation stress short-term earnings often to the detriment of long-term profits, and though neither is technically illegal, they have attracted the interest of government regulators from the U.S. Securities and Exchange Commission (Whoriskey & Gottlieb, 2019). Agency theory and familiness (Duréndez & Madrid-Guijarro, 2018) along with social embeddedness theory (Gao et al., 2021) are conceptual approaches that have been employed to examine earnings management (and manipulation) and its use by a family in attempting to maintain control of the family firm.

A common subject of study in accounting, earnings management has been the focus of only a few studies involving family firms with mixed results. Gao et al., (2021) studied Chinese family firms and found they engaged in more aggressive earnings management when ownership is concentrated in the family. Earnings management occurs in the social context of the family, where family members are entrenched in executive positions, enabling the family to disguise the firm's actual performance and protect their controlling position. This was not the case in other studies of small family firms, where multigenerational ownership and management, as well as strong shared values, resulted in higher quality earnings, that is, earnings not manipulated to achieve a desired reporting figure (Avabruth & Padhi, 2023; Duréndez & Madrid-Guijarro, 2018).

Other forms of financial misconduct that risk hurting financial performance of family firms include insider trading (Anderson et al., 2012), intermingling of funds (Yilmazer & Schrank, 2006), and poor internal controls (Bardhan et al., 2015). Anderson et al. (2012) studied short sales for family firms, finding an unusually high level of such trading just before negative earnings announcements. This implies that family members and their networks engage in shorting (an individual sells a stock effective at a future date at the current price confident the stock will decline in price by the future date after the negative earnings report becomes public. The individual buys the stock at that future date and pockets the difference). Although this practice potentially indicates insider trading, insider trading is not studied explicitly in the research.

Insider trading is clearly illegal, but intermingling may not be even though it does not represent good corporate governance. Yilmazer and Schrank (2010) distinguished bootstrapping, where the owners support the family firm with personal resources, from intermingling, when business resources are used for the family's personal benefit. Extreme examples of intermingling such as Adelphia Communications (Kidwell, 2008) and Parmalat (Mevorach, 2012) demonstrate potentially catastrophic outcomes for external stockholders as well as survival of the family business. However, in a study of family firms, Yilmazer and Schrank (2006) found they were no more likely than non-family firms to engage in intermingling, after controlling for characteristics of the business and the household.

Financial management that harms profitability is not necessarily misconduct, per se, but to the extent that it exists, the family is not exercising its full fiduciary duty to external shareholders. One such example of financial management is top management team pay dispersion, where there is a significant spread in compensation among members of the team, potentially resulting in lower firm performance (Jaskiewicz et al., 2017). However, this may not necessarily represent dysfunction, as the family must balance financial performance against competing familial needs. Those alternate needs appear to take on less importance in subsequent generations, however, when top management pay dispersion decreases.

Internal control over financial reporting represents another potentially dysfunctional financial management issue in family firms. After the collapse of Enron, World Com, Adelphia Communications, and others, the Sarbanes Oxley Act required a new emphasis on internal controls over financial reporting. Beginning in 2004, publicly traded companies in the United States were required to report material weaknesses in those controls. Bardhan et al. (2015) found that S&P 500 family firms were more likely to have material weaknesses reported, especially if dual-class shares enabled the family to have greater board representation than their percentage ownership of the business would suggest.

4.3 Bribery/Corruption

> For the past several months, South Korea has been roiled by accusations of corruption in its government and major businesses. The role of the country's family-run businesses, and whether or how they are held to account for wrongdoing, is under intense scrutiny. In February Samsung's de facto leader Lee Jae-yong was arrested on bribery charges. Lee is accused of donating $36 million to nonprofit foundations operated by a friend of the former president in return for political favors...Then in March, South Korea's president, Park Geun-hye, was removed from office, in part because of accusations that she helped a friend, Choi Soon-sil, pressure companies into making donations to non-profit organizations controlled by Choi and gave her access to secret government documents. The outrage at these and similar scandals helped propel liberal candidate Moon Jae-in to the presidency; he campaigned on promises to clamp down on the country's family-controlled business dynasties in the wake of Park's cronyism and corruption scandal. Many South Koreans feel envy and resentment toward family-run conglomerates such as Samsung, SK, LG, and Hyundai. Known as *chaebol,* these businesses make up more than half the value of the companies traded on South Korea's stock exchange. However, their contribution to the world's 11th-largest economy is overshadowed by repeated cases of bribery, weak corporate governance, and complicated shareholding plans that help the families accumulate wealth and inherit management. (Most of the chaebol are in their third generation of family control.) Moon has vowed to stop families from using such methods to keep control of these ostensibly public companies. (Chun, 2017)

The corruption of Samsung and its fellow chaebol and the long history of Siemens's global bribery strategy—in particular, paying off officials across four continents to secure government contracts in the 2000s (French, n.d.)—indicate that many prominent family firms practice high stakes dysfunctional behavior around the world. Sometimes they are caught and punished. Corporate corruption is an issue with both family and non-family firms and most research into bribery and corruption compares the two. There are some signs that researchers are starting to examine bribery and corruption across family firms, opening the possibility that heterogeneity in family firms in terms of degree, antecedents, and results of these differences can be delineated.

For now, several comparisons on bribery and corruption between family and non-family businesses can be noted. In contrast with non-family firms, family firms were found to be more susceptible to corruption in Eastern Europe. As a result, the export share of family businesses, compared to non-family firms, was more positively associated with informal payments aimed to facilitate business operations (Bassetti et al., 2015). However, because family firms are motivated to protect their socioemotional wealth (SEW) by avoiding actions that could damage their reputations and other non-economic factors, they are expected to be less likely to pay bribes than non-family firms.

One study found that in countries with a weaker governance environment, family-controlled firms are indeed less likely to engage in bribery because of the damage this behavior would do to the family firm's image (Ding et al., 2016). Differences between family and non-family firms were not found in countries with more established and transparent governance mechanisms. Yet, pursuit of SEW may both encourage and dissuade family firms' willingness to engage in bribery (Jiang & Min, 2022) depending on whether the type of SEW benefits are more family centric such as providing permanent job security to family members or are more likely to provide benefits that go beyond the family such as contributing to the community or forming long-term partnerships with non-family interests. Jiang and Min (2022) found that family management may have an inverted-U shape relationship with bribery that increases when family firms gain political power and decreases when corruption is being investigated. When family firms enter countries with higher levels of corruption, they are more likely to choose greenfield investment (building operations from the ground up) and full ownership rather than share the ownership with local entities (Yamanoi & Asaba, 2018). An SEW perspective would suggest that greater control over foreign subsidiaries is needed to restrict corrupt behaviors that could damage the family firm's SEW and its reputation (Yamanoi and Asaba (2018).

Perceptions of the business environment and the prevailing culture can also exert different influences on the bribery and corruption views of family firm leaders. In a sample of 310 privately held small and medium-sized enterprises (SMEs) from 22 transition economies, Eddleston and colleagues (2020) discovered a bribery paradox in that entrepreneurs who pay frequent bribes perceive they have greater long-term business obstacles. Family leaders were found to be especially vulnerable to the danger of perceiving these obstacles growing over time, resulting in a "new normal" obstacle-ridden business environment as their bribery frequency increased due to their tendency to view bribes through the family's perspective.

In China, due to a lack of legal safeguards, family firms use their political connections to protect private property rights. Tang et al. (2013) found that political participation is an active response to the failure of the legal system to adequately defend private property rights and thus to support the rapid growth of the family firm. Finally, cultural differences of virtues and ethics among family firms are based on Western (Aristotelian) versus Eastern (Confucian) traditions, which explains why views of bribery, gift-giving, and nepotism diverge and are seen as unethical by some family firms and acceptable by others (Sison et al., 2020).

4.4 Corporate Social Irresponsibility/ Environmental Performance

Corporate Social Responsibility (CSR)—a form of private business self-regulation that tries to contribute to societal goals by using philanthropy, community engagement, ethical conduct, and sustainable business practices—has been a frequent research interest in the family business literature with a recent review identifying more than 160 studies on the topic (Mariani et al., 2023). At this stage, CSR has become the norm of international businesses, and many family businesses that fail to engage in CSR practices indicate deviance by the family firm and potentially dysfunctional outcomes for stakeholders. Beyond failing to engage at all is the possibility that a firm might act in a way that would be regarded as irresponsible from a CSR standpoint.

Research related to CSR considers the importance of the external environment in determining whether firms—both family and non-family—act ethically or unethically. Contrasting examples include the lower likelihood of family firms using tax havens when internationalizing (Temouri et al., 2022), and the lower environmental performance of family firms unless they are socially embedded in the community (Dekker & Hasso, 2016). Block and Wagner (2014) found that family ownership is negatively associated with community-related CSR performance, but positively associated with diversity-, employee-, environment- and product-related aspects of CSR. Thus, family firms may demonstrate greater levels of CSR, attempting to maintain a positive reputation because the family can more easily be identified as owners—perhaps their family name is on the sign out front.

Results are decidedly mixed as to how family firms fare when it comes to CSR. Cruz et al. (2014) found that family firms can be both socially responsible and irresponsible simultaneously because national standards and industry conditions influence the degree of CSR in non-family firms and less so in family businesses. Cabeza-Garcia et al. (2017) found that family ownership and governance were negatively related to CSR disclosure. However, the presence of foreign investors reduced the negative effects of family ownership, while the presence of other families increased the negative impact of family governance on CSR disclosure. Depending on the family's involvement in management, boards of directors can be functional or dysfunctional. When the board includes outside directors with equity ownership and diverse educational backgrounds, CSR engagement increases among professionally managed firms, but decreases among family-managed firms (Oh et al., 2019). A negative relationship between family ownership and CSR may be stronger when the firms belong to groups with larger, more influential business networks and more charitable foundations (Oh et al., 2022).

Most of the extant studies on environmental performance focus on differences between family and non-family firms and link back to the antecedents discussed in Chapter 2, but in some cases with positive effects. For example, because of concerns for socioemotional wealth, family firms have stronger environmental performance than non-family firms (Berrone et al., 2010). Kim et al. (2017) found family firms to be more environmentally responsible and less likely to greenwash, i.e., provide misleading information to hide environmental abuse and maintain a positive reputation, than non-family firms. Their study found that family firms positively moderated the relationship between top managers' attention to natural environmental issues and environmental action, whereas non-family firms showed less environmental activity as their purported attention to environmental issues increased, suggesting that greenwashing was taking place. Finally, Terlaak and colleagues (2018) found that family control affects environmental performance disclosure based on whether the firm has a family member CEO and the level of family ownership. There is a greater likelihood to reveal the company's environmental performance when family control of a business group is more extensive, suggesting that family leadership combined with family ownership—a condition often linked to inefficiencies and fraud in business groups—can be used to encourage responsible behaviors as well.

However, positive comparisons are countered by a meta-analysis of family firm environmental performance indicating that family involvement may have a small, but negative relationship to a firm's environmental performance (Miroshnychenko et al., 2022). A cynical view is that family firms engage in corporate philanthropy to shift the focus away from their firms' environmental misconduct. Corporate environmental misconduct is positively and significantly associated with corporate philanthropic giving, and the positive association is less pronounced for politically connected family-owned firms than for their counterparts (Du, 2015).

In sum, what drives CSR as a popular topic in the family firm realm, generally focused on the relationship between CSR and family engagement or the impact of CSR on family firm performance, whereas the negative elements of family firm involvement with CSR and with environmental performance across family firms have received less consideration. To address the heterogeneity of family firms on these topics, additional study of areas that drive CSR adoption (firm features, family involvement, corporate governance, socioemotional wealth, ethics, and religion) (Mariani et al., 2023) should continue to guide the investigation of the dysfunctional aspects of family firm corporate social irresponsibility and poor environmental performance.

4.5 Tax Avoidance/Tax Evasion

Fraud, as discussed earlier, often manifests itself amid accusations that the family firm has evaded paying its taxes (e.g., Marritz et al., 2023). But there are differences in what is considered legal and not legal when it comes to any individual's or business's stance on paying taxes to the government: Did they evade or avoid? Most of the research thus far has considered avoidance and aggressiveness rather than evasion.

More than 20 papers have been published in the last 12 years that focus on family firms and variations of tax avoidance—including tax aggressiveness, tax evasion, and tax "heaven"—according to a recent review (Khelil & Khlif, 2022). The review indicated important differences in how family businesses view tax avoidance across the countries that were studied—mainly Germany, United States, Taiwan, several developing countries (e.g., Brazil, India), and European civil law countries such as Belgium and France. The association between family firms and tax avoidance was negative in the United States, Finland, and Belgium. The relationship was positive and significant in developed (Germany and Italy) and developing economies (Brazil, India, Malaysia. and Tunisia) (Khelil & Khlif, 2022). Interestingly, very few of these studies focused on evasion with most considering aggressiveness and avoidance.

The evasion/avoidance distinction is particularly important when it is framed in the context of deviance and dysfunction. If it is a societal norm that people should seek to pay as little taxes as legally possible, then the family firm, as any other taxpayer, who engages in tax aggressiveness or avoidance by seeking legally to lower the tax liability, is not being deviant. In societies in which it is *not* the prevailing norm to seek to pay less taxes (wherever that is!), then the family firm who practiced tax avoidance would be considered deviant. However, when the family firm uses illegal means to not pay its required taxes, it would be engaging in deviant behavior as the codification of tax law establishes a norm regarding how illegal conduct, i.e., evasion, regarding taxes is viewed. In terms of whether tax avoidance and tax evasion are dysfunctional, it can be argued that they are both dysfunctional to the government, which uses the tax money ostensibly to provide services to its citizens and would have less to spend and have to raise taxes or cut programs if less revenue is collected. However, either scenario of paying less taxes—legal or illegal—might not be seen as dysfunctional by family firm members—unless they face criminal or civil charges for evasion or are shamed in public for violating a societal norm against tax avoidance. Either way the family firm's brand is potentially tarnished whether the leaders acted illegally or not.

As noted, previous research has focused largely on aggressiveness and avoidance rather than evasion. In general, family firms were found to be less tax aggressive than non-family firms (Brune et al., 2019a, 2019b; Chen et al., 2010; Steijvers & Niskanen, 2014; Temouri et al., 2022) with some conditions such as being a privately held rather than publicly traded company. This relationship of lower tax avoidance by family firms was guided in some cases by a desire to maintain family reputation (Chen et al., 2010) or socioemotional wealth (Brune et al, 2019a; Cao et al., 2023) or is linked to corporate social responsibility reporting (Itan & Artamevia, 2022; Yopie & Elivia, 2022; Özbay et al., 2023).

Some of the research into tax avoidance and evasion indicates differences across family firms when it comes to being aggressive about paying less taxes. For example, family firms, although less tax avoidant than non-family firms, are more tax aggressive when there is a lower share of CEO ownership. But the presence of an outside director on the board lessens this effect (Steijvers & Niskanen, 2014). Tax aggressiveness differed among family firms when levels of family involvement were considered: Family control and management were found to lessen tax aggressiveness while the inclusion of second and subsequent generations in the family firm was linked to higher levels of tax aggressiveness (Sanchez-Marin et al., 2016). Eddleston and Mulki (2021) connected the strength of a family firm's identity to tax evasion in that family firm identity is negatively related to tax evasion when firm performance is high, but when firm performance is low, family firm identity is positively related to tax evasion. Finally, private family and private non-family firms may not differ in their levels of tax avoidance unless the private family firm is wholly owned and managed by family members, in which case the firms engage in less tax avoidance (Brune et al., 2019b).

The next step in this line of research would be to investigate how family businesses, economies, and culture are different in the countries in which family firms tend to pursue tax avoidance more than others. Such studies would help identify this behavior as deviant and/or dysfunctional depending on the context.

4.6 Concluding Comments

When looking at the heterogeneity of family firms, several differences emerge when the dysfunctional (or deviant) behaviors that extend from the family firm outside the business are examined. Fraud, financial misconduct, bribery, corruption, corporate social irresponsibility, environmental performance, tax avoidance, and tax evasion have the potential to damage external stakeholders such as customers, competitors, regulators, government, and society at large. Some of these behaviors can benefit the family firm, at least in the short term, while containing dysfunctional elements that can damage others (fraud, bribery), and some of the behaviors might not be considered to be dysfunctional or deviant at all (e.g., earnings management, tax avoidance).

Although much of the current research on these topics contrasts family firms with non-family firms, several more recent studies have considered differences across family firms in the areas of fraud (e.g., Guo et al., 2022), financial misconduct (e.g., Ding & Wu, 2014), bribery (e.g., Jiang & Min, 2022), corruption (e.g., Tang et al., 2013), corporate social irresponsibility (Oh et al., 2019), tax avoidance (e.g., Steijvers & Niskanen, 2014), and tax evasion (e.g., Eddleston & Mulki, 2021).

More so than dysfunctional behavior within the family firm, the types of actions discussed in this chapter often make headlines and have strong implications for the future of the family business when their specific and significant foibles in areas such as fraud, corruption, and negative environmental performance are exposed by the media and by the justice system. Some of these family organizations (Samsung, Siemens) are established enough, large enough, and financially strong enough to continue to thrive once hit by these accusations. Others such as British parking services owner Mohammed Isaq, who was sentenced to a year and a half in prison for fraud and banned from running any business for six years (Tooth, 2023), do not.

Yet, some of the research suggests that despite what happens in the court of public opinion and the court of law, some family firms attempt to compensate for past wrongdoing—or at least polish their image—by being more socially responsible. Their actions in this regard are indicated by studies that find a positive association between family firm corporate misconduct and philanthropic giving (Du, 2015) and a negative association between tax avoidance and social/environmental performance (Lopez-Gonzalez et al., 2019). Discussion of the outcomes of dysfunction and deviance on such matters as family firm performance and company reputation are the subject of the next chapter.

References

Anderson, R., Martin, G. S., & Reeb, D. (2017). *Financial misconduct and family firms* (Working Paper). Temple University

Anderson, R. C., Reeb, D. M., & Zhao, W. (2012). Family-controlled firms and informed trading: Evidence from short sales. *The Journal of Finance, 67*(1), 351–385.

Avabruth, S. M., & Padhi, S. K. (2023). Earnings management by family firms to meet the debt covenants: Evidence from India. *Journal of Accounting in Emerging Economies, 13*(1), 93–117.

Bardhan, I., Lin, S., & Wu, S. L. (2015). The quality of internal control over financial reporting in family firms. *Accounting Horizons, 29*(1), 41–60.

Bassetti, T., Maso, L., & Lattanzi, N. (2015). Family businesses in Eastern European countries: How informal payments affect exports. *Journal of Family Business Strategy, 6*, 219–233.

Berrone, P., Cruz, C., Gomez-Mejia, L., & Larraza-Kintana, M. (2010). Socioemotional wealth and corporate responses to institutional pressures: Do family-controlled firms pollute less? *Administrative Sciences, 55*, 82–113.

Block, J., & Wagner, M. (2014). The effect of family ownership on different dimensions of corporate social responsibility: Evidence from large US firms. *Business Strategy and the Environment, 23*, 475–492.

Brune, A., Thomsen, M., & Watrin, C. (2019a). Family firm heterogeneity and tax avoidance: The role of the founder. *Family Business Review, 32*(3), 296–317.

Brune, A., Thomsen, M., & Watrin, C. (2019b). Tax avoidance in different firm types and the role of nonfamily involvement in private family firms. *Managerial and Decision Economics, 40*(8), 950–970.

Cabeza-Garcia, L., Sacristan-Navarro, M., & Gomez-Anson, S. (2017). Family involvement and corporate social responsibility disclosure. *Journal of Family Business Strategy, 9*, 109–122.

Cao, F., Li, S., Dai, M., & Li, J. (2023). Your heart is where your treasure is: Family chairman and tax avoidance in family-controlled firms. *Journal of Business Research, 154*, 113298.

Chen, S., Chen, X., Cheng, Q., & Shevlin, T. (2010). Are family firms more tax aggressive than non-family firms? *Journal of Financial Economics, 95*(1), 41–61.

Chun, R. (2017). Samsung, shame, and corporate atonement. *Harvard Business Review*. Retrieved October 10, 2023 from https://hbr.org/2017/05/samsung-shame-and-corporate-atonement

Cressey, D. R. (1953). *Other people's money*. The Free Press.

Cruz, C., Larraza-Kintana, M., Garces-Galdeano, L., & Berrone, P. (2014). Are family firms really more socially responsible? *Entrepreneurship Theory and Practice, 38*(6), 1295–1316.

Dekker, J., & Hasso, T. (2016). Environmental performance focus in private family firms: The role of social embeddedness. *Journal of Business Ethics, 136*, 293–309.

Ding, S., Qu, B., & Wu, Z. (2016). Family control, socioemotional wealth, and governance environment: The case of bribes. *Journal of Business Ethics, 136*(3), 639–654.

Ding, S., & Wu, Z. (2014). Family ownership and corporate misconduct in U.S. small firms. *Journal of Business Ethics, 123*(2), 183–195.
Du, X. (2015). Is corporate philanthropy used as environmental misconduct dressing? Evidence from Chinese family-owned firms. *Journal of Business Ethics, 129*, 341–361.
Duréndez, A., & Madrid-Guijarro, A. (2018). The impact of family influence on financial reporting quality in small and medium family firms. *Journal of Family Business Strategy, 9*(3), 205–218.
Eddleston, K., Banalieva, E., & Verbeke, A. (2020). The bribery paradox in transition economies and the enactment of 'new normal' business environments. *Journal of Management Studies, 57*(3), 597–625.
Eddleston, K., & Mulki, J. (2021). Differences in family-owned SMEs' ethical behavior: A mixed gamble perspective of family firm tax evasion. *Entrepreneurship Theory and Practice, 45*(4), 767–791.
French, L. (n.d.). *A history of corporate bribery scandals*. World Finance. Retrieved October 10, 2023 from https://www.worldfinance.com/strategy/a-history-of-bribery
Gao, J., Masli, A., Suh, I., & Xu, J. (2021). The influence of a family business climate and CEO–CFO relationship quality on misreporting conduct. *Journal of Business Ethics, 171*(1), 99–122.
Ghafoor, A., Zainudin, R., & Mahdzan, N. S. (2019a). Corporate fraud and information asymmetry in emerging markets: Case of firms subject to enforcement actions in Malaysia. *Journal of Financial Crime, 26*(1), 95–112.
Ghafoor, A., Zainudin, R., & Mahdzan, N. S. (2019b). Factors eliciting corporate fraud in emerging markets: Case of firms subject to enforcement actions in Malaysia. *Journal of Business Ethics, 160*(2), 587–608.
Gottschalk, P., & Asting, C. (2019). The family firm as an arena for white-collar crime. *International Journal of Business Continuity and Risk Management, 9*(4), 283–297.
Gottschalk, P. (2020). Theory of convenience: Determinants of white-collar crime intention. *Deviant Behavior, 41*(11), 1431–1439.
Guo, Y., Luo, X. R., & Li, D. (2022). Hierarchical inconsistency: A monitoring mechanism to reduce securities fraud in emerging markets. *Organization Science, 33*(6), 2187–2208.
Itan, I., & Artamevia, N. (2022). Effect of family ownership, corporate social responsibility, on tax avoidance: Moderating effect of audit quality. *SEIKO: Journal of Management & Business, 4*(3), 631–641.
Jaskiewicz, P., Block, J. H., Miller, D., & Combs, J. G. (2017). Founder versus family owners' impact on pay dispersion among non-CEO top managers: Implications for firm performance. *Journal of Management, 43*(5), 1524–1552.

Jiang, S., & Min, Y. (2022). The ability and willingness of family firms to bribe: A socioemotional wealth perspective. *Journal of Business Ethics*. https://doi.org/10.1007/s10551-022-05086-1

Khelil, I., & Khlif, H. (2022). Tax avoidance in family firms: A literature review. *Journal of Financial Crime*. https://doi.org/10.1108/JFC-03-2022-0064

Kidwell, R. E. (2008). Adelphia Communications: The public company that became a private piggy bank: A case of fraud in the Rigas family firm. In S. Matulich & D. Currie (Eds.), *Handbook of frauds, scams, and swindles: Failures of ethics in leadership* (pp. 191–205). Taylor and Francis Group.

Kidwell, R. E., Eddleston, K. A., Kidwell, L. A., Cater, J. J., & Howard, E. (2023). *Dysfunctional behavior in family firms across individuals, families, firms, and environments* (Unpublished Working Paper).

Kim, J., Fairclough, S., & Dibrell, C. (2017). Attention, action, and greenwash in family-influenced firms? Evidence from polluting industries. *Organization & Environment, 30*(4), 304–323.

Krishnan, G., & Peytcheva, M. (2019). The risk of fraud in family firms: Assessments of external auditors. *Journal of Business Ethics, 157*(1), 261–278.

Lopez-Gonzalez, E., Martinez-Ferrero, J., & Garcia-Meca, E. (2019). Does corporate social responsibility affect tax avoidance: Evidence from family firms. *Corporate Social Responsibility & Environmental Management, 26*(4), 819–831.

Mariani, M. M., Al-Sultan, K., & De Massis, A. (2023). Corporate social responsibility in family firms: A systematic literature review. *Journal of Small Business Management, 61*(3), 1192–1246.

Marritz, I., Bernstein, A., & Mann, B. (2023, January 13). *The Trump Organization has been ordered to pay $1.61 million for tax fraud*. National Public Radio. Retrieved October 11, 2023 from https://www.npr.org/2023/01/13/1148379013/the-trump-organization-has-been-ordered-to-pay-1-61-million-for-tax-fraud

Mevorach, I. (2012). INSOL Europe's proposals on groups of companies (in cross-border insolvency): A critical appraisal. *International Insolvency Review, 21*(3), 183–197.

Miroshnychenko, I., De Massis, A., Barontini, R., & Testa, F. (2022). Family firms and environmental performance: A meta-analytic review. *Family Business Review, 35*(1), 68–90.

Nilakantan, R., Iyengar, D., Datta, S. K., & Rao, S. (2021). On ethical violations in microfinance backed small businesses: Family and household welfare. *Journal of Business Ethics, 172*(4), 785–802.

Ning, Y. P. (2009). The theoretical framework of earnings management. *Canadian Social Science, 1*(3), 32–38.

Oh, W.-Y., Chang, Y. K., & Jung, R. (2019). Board characteristics and corporate social responsibility: Does family involvement in management matter? *Journal of Business Research, 103*, 23–33.
Oh, W.-Y., Ree, H., Chang, Y. K., & Postuła, I. (2022). Trees in the forest: How do family owners make CSR decisions in business groups? *Journal of Business Ethics, 187*(4), 759–780.
Özbay, D., Adıgüzel, H., & Karahan Gökmen, M. (2023). Corporate social responsibility and tax avoidance: Channeling effect of family firms. *Journal of Corporate Accounting & Finance*. https://doi.org/10.1002/jcaf.22610
Sanchez-Marin, G., Portillo-Navarro, M., & Clavel, J. (2016). The influence of family involvement on tax aggressiveness of family firms. *Journal of Family Business Management, 6*(2), 143–168.
Sison, A., Ferrero, I., & Redin, D. (2020). Some virtue ethics implications from Aristotelian and Confucian perspectives on family and business. *Journal of Business Ethics, 165*, 241–254.
Snyder, N. H., Broome, O. W., & Zimmerman, K. (1989). Using internal controls to reduce employee theft in small businesses. *Journal of Small Business Management, 27*(3), 48.
Steijvers, T., & Niskanen, M. (2014). Tax aggressiveness in private family firms: An agency perspective. *Journal of Family Business Strategy, 5*(4), 347–357.
Tang, Y., Ye, S., & Zhou, J. (2013). Political connections, legal environment, and corporate valuation in Chinese public family firms. *The Chinese Economy, 46*(6), 32–49.
Temouri, Y., Nardella, G., Jones, C., & Brammer, S. (2022). Haven-sent? Tax havens, corporate social irresponsibility and the dark side of family firm internationalization. *British Journal of Management, 33*(3), 1447–1467.
Terlaak, A., Kim, S., & Roh, T. (2018). Not good, not bad: The effect of family control on environmental performance disclosure by business group firms. *Journal of Business Ethics, 153*, 977–996.
Tooth, J. (2023). *Fraudsters sentenced for scam Manchester Airport parking*. Messenger Newspapers. https://www.messengernewspapers.co.uk/news/23761474.fraudsters-sentenced-scam-manchester-airport-Parking/?utm_source=ground.news&utm_medium=referral
Turner, L. E., & Weirich, T. R. (2006). A closer look at financial statement restatements. *The CPA Journal, 76*(12), 12.
Walker, A. (2023). How a family firm that sold a pipe dream for holidaymakers spiralled out of control. *Manchester Evening News*. Retrieved October 10, 2023 from https://www.manchestereveningnews.co.uk/news/greater-manchester-news/how-family-firm-sold-pipe-27623328
Whoriskey, N. & Gottlieb, C. (2019). SEC cracks down on earnings management. *Harvard Law School Forum on Corporate Governance*, December 17.

Retrieved June 15, 2022 from https://corpgov.law.harvard.edu/2019/12/17/sec-cracks-down-on-earnings-management/

Yamanoi, J., & Asaba, S. (2018). The impact of family ownership on establishment and ownership modes in foreign direct investment: The moderating role of corruption in host countries. *Global Strategy Journal, 8*, 106–135.

Yilmazer, T., & Schrank, H. (2006). Financial intermingling in small family businesses. *Journal of Business Venturing, 21*(5), 726–751.

Yilmazer, T., & Schrank, H. (2010). The use of owner resources in small and family owned businesses: Literature review and future research directions. *Journal of Family and Economic Issues, 31*(4), 399–413.

Yopie, S., & Elivia, E. (2022). The effect of corporate social responsibility, family ownership on tax avoidance: The effect of audit quality moderation. *Indonesian Journal of Economics, Social, and Humanities, 4*(1), 29–40.

CHAPTER 5

Differential Impacts of Dysfunction and Deviance

Abstract The effects of deviant and dysfunctional behaviors on family firms as well as individuals, families, and external stakeholders are examined. The areas in which the impact of deviant and dysfunctional behaviors are discussed include firm performance, succession processes, governance, firm reputation, and business-family relationships. Family firms can be locked into a vicious circle of negative behaviors based upon the way that dysfunctional acts are managed within the firm; a circle that can end in dissolution of the firm and isolation from the family. However, constructive and strategic deviance offer opportunities for positive outcomes. The chapter discusses how the effects of deviance and dysfunction can do a family firm "good" and a society "bad"—and sometimes benefit both.

Keywords Family firms · Firm performance · Succession · Reputation · Brand · Family relationships · Constructive deviance · Strategic deviance

Deviant and dysfunctional behavior in the family firm is logically associated with negative outcomes for individuals, families, family firms, and external stakeholders. Targeted family members are physically and emotionally damaged by acts of aggression such as bullying. Family firms

R. E. Kidwell, *Dysfunction and Deviance Across Family Firms*, Palgrave Studies in Family Business Heterogeneity,
https://doi.org/10.1007/978-3-031-51816-4_5

are hurt financially when employees steal resources from them, or when family and non-family members alike reduce the effort they put into their work. The physical environment suffers as family firms engage in socially irresponsible, unethical, and sometimes illegal behavior. Taxpayers are called on to make up for the deficit in government revenues caused by family firms' evasion and avoidance of taxes. Family firm leaders might go to prison to pay for their fraud while thousands of employees lose their jobs as the company becomes insolvent.

For example, Adelphia Communications Corp. founder John Rigas and his son Timothy were convicted of conspiracy, bank fraud, and securities fraud for looting the cable company and duping its investors. John Rigas, 79, and Timothy Rigas, 47, faced 30 years in prison on the most serious charge, bank fraud (Bull, 2004). Despite maintaining their innocence, both father and son ended up spending several years in federal prison, and the business the Rigas family had built over many years was quickly destroyed (Beauge, 2023).

Repercussions caused by family firm dysfunctional behavior can be long lasting. Parmalat, Europe's biggest corporate fraud, cost investors billions of euros and ensnared many of the world's largest investment banks. The scandal was still reverberating with lawsuits 15 years after it was found that the Italian dairy business had cooked its books for more than a decade. Parmalat filed for bankruptcy after it was revealed that a company bank account in the Cayman Islands holding €4 billion ($4.5 billion) didn't exist. An audit found the firm had overstated sales and profits for over a decade and had a debt that was eight times more than declared. More than a dozen executives wound up in jail, and police caught one executive smashing a computer hard drive with a hammer, trying to destroy evidence (Sylvers, 2019).

Despite these extreme outcomes, the results of some externally directed behaviors can have differential effects such as corporate social irresponsibility and a family firm's environmental performance. As noted in the previous chapter, negative acts can be positive for some family firms—at least in the short term—because the firms and their managers are primarily the perpetrators of these acts rather than the targets. This could also be the case regarding dysfunction and deviance within the firm in the sense that (1) bifurcation bias benefits competent (and incompetent) family members at non-family employees' expense, (2) family members who shirk responsibilities usually continue in their jobs and thus—playing on parental guilt—perceive greater levels of entitlement and behave even more poorly, and (3) mistreated non-family employees who seek justice in enacting revenge by stealing from the firm keep their ill-gotten gains—unless they are caught.

Although there are potential short-term positives for the perpetrators and definite negatives for the targets, the diversity of outcomes associated with these usually "negative" behaviors shows that deviance in the family and family firm can have positive and constructive results depending on the nature of the norms that are being broken and the nature of the deviance that is taking place. Dysfunction can also serve a strategic function to the family and the family firm, but as will be seen later, the ethical nature of this form of dysfunction is sometimes questionable.

This chapter summarizes the heterogeneous impact of deviant and dysfunctional behavior in family firms—inside and outside—negative and positive. The chapter discusses implications and outcomes for firm performance, succession, and governance processes in the family business and the business family, reputation and brand of the family and the family firm, and business family relationships—and how some family firms address them. Finally, the positive and strategic aspects of deviance and dysfunction are elaborated.

5.1 Firm Performance

Dysfunctional behavior within the family firm has the potential to hurt not only the targets but can create collateral damage to co-workers and the firm itself, even if it is not a target. For example, forms of gender discrimination among the rank and file, which can include sexual harassment of employees—family and non-family alike—can result in liability to the family firm in terms of lawsuits and other legal actions. These behaviors have strong potential to hinder the firm's financial performance as well as its ability to hire outside talent.

When a family member is not punished for committing offenses at work that would not be tolerated if committed by non-family members, a feeling of injustice can arise among those other employees, or even by other family members who are working hard and playing by the rules. This could have negative effects on individual and team efforts and performance and ultimately hurt the organization. Other employees may withdraw from providing their full effort, or they may start engaging in dysfunctional behaviors of their own. Bad behavior on the part of a family member may also affect how the offending family member is treated—possibly the family firm leader will feel guilt and make bad choices, such as giving the family member a pay raise in a misguided attempt to mitigate their future behavior. Offenders may see this as validation of their behavior and continue down the same path or consider the reward an endorsement of their business savvy. This could create problems if incompetent family members are positioned to make important decisions for the family firm; they will likely be bad decisions (Kidwell et al., 2013).

Previous research indicates that firm-level conflict can either encourage family firms to face situations where issues can be resolved to improve firm performance, or it can break and divide families (Hoelscher, 2014). Firm-level conflict—including agency conflict (Blanco-Mazagatos et al., 2016), quarreling due to the complex ownership structures over multiple generations (Sacristan-Navarro & Cabeza-Garcia, 2019), and disputes over the forming of family firm factions (Minichilli et al., 2010)—is just one of the dysfunctional behaviors that drive or moderate damage to family firm performance. Others include bifurcation bias (Jennings et al., 2018), favoritism/nepotism (Hudson et al., 2019; Schmid & Sender, 2021), and gender discrimination (Jain et al., 2021). For example, biased decisions against non-family employees may lead these employees to decrease their effort levels, lower satisfaction with their jobs, and ultimately leave the company. All these responses by non-family members may hurt the firm's productivity and harm the expense side of the ledger as the firm would have to spend money to find replacements for employees who leave—and then train the new recruits. These factors can have a negative economic impact on various stakeholders including employees, customers, and investors. In addition, perceptions of gender discrimination regarding family members and non-family members may limit the available talent to take positions in the firm. Next-generation daughters may not seek employment in the family firm due to its gender norms, and this talent loss could lead to less-than-optimal firm performance (Overbeke et al., 2013).

5.2 Firm Succession/Governance

If female family members decide not to pursue leadership roles in their family businesses due to gender norms or perceived discrimination, this outcome has potential to negatively impact the succession process for family firm leaders who wish to pass the baton to the next generation

(Ahrens et al., 2015). Other types of behaviors within the firm such as interpersonal conflict that damages interactions in the succession process (Handler, 1991) can also hurt a family firm's plan for its future. But there can be varying results that ultimately lead to a successful generational turnover of leadership depending on how the process is managed, who the players are, and their level of involvement (Ahrens et al., 2018).

The first place to look in terms of dysfunction's impact on succession is the degree of firm-level conflict and how it is affecting the process. Surfacing and resolving the conflict is key to avoiding unsuccessful outcomes, and some family firms have seen positive results by using teams of successors rather than a designated individual (Cater & Kidwell, 2014; Cater et al., 2016). A qualitative study of nine family firms found that destructive competition in a successor group hurt its effectiveness as successors whereas increased trust, agreement to share power, and a general pattern of cooperation in a successor group resulted in positive outcomes (Cater & Kidwell, 2014). However, disagreements resulting from earlier interactions among family members can lead to serious relationship conflict that can escalate to firm-level conflict among siblings, for example, resulting in disbanding of the successor group and eventually dissolution of the firm (Cater et al, 2016). These authors identified both a positive and a negative track for team succession illustrating the heterogeneous nature of dysfunction's effects on the succession process.

The differential effects of dysfunction can also be seen by considering firm-level conflicts within the context of corporate and family governance. Researchers have documented instances where large scale, cross generational conflict has developed that proved very damaging to the family firm. For example, El Corte Inglés, a fourth-generation, Spanish family-owned firm that started as a small tailor's shop and grew into a diversified venture that includes department stores, hypermarkets, and a travel agency, suffered severe cross generational family conflict (Sacristan-Navarro & Cabeza-Garcia, 2019) Unfortunately, the company's ownership structure was ridden with conflicts of interest between traditional family shareholders and new ones (family and non-family), and between family shareholders who were managing the company and those who were not. The diversity of ownership that included multiple generations and non-family members led to haggling over the valuation of the stock and to shareholder wars in which family shareholders were accused of improperly influencing the board of directors. These matters became very public as some of the parties filed lawsuits during the dispute.

However, corporate governance mechanisms that can be implemented before trouble arrives lead to very different solutions across family firms who are experiencing a serious level of conflict, whether it be internal disagreement or conflicts of interest. The problems of El Corte Inglés are grounded in family business research on corporate governance and could be addressed in several ways: establishing a family council that would keep contentious conversation inside the family and out of the public eye, implementing a family constitution that spells out agreement on what to do in case of a dispute among family members, and going public to allow valuation of shares to take place and providing an outlet for family members to sell their shares on the open market (Sacristan-Navarro & Cabeza-Garcia, 2019). Family firms that take these steps will lessen the impact of firm-level conflict among family and non-family alike; they are wise to move from self-governance and family governance to corporate governance before disputes arise.

Purkayastha et al. (2019, 2022) focused on structural mechanisms to temper the effects of agency conflicts—specifically Type 1 (principal-agent) and Type 2 (principal-principal), the latter of which particularly plagues family firms as the dominant shareholder group's interests (e.g., family) may differ from those of other shareholders. While increasing the family's ownership control reduces the extent of Type 1 agency conflicts (between the family owners and the non-family managers), it leads to more Type 2 agency conflicts (between family and non-family owners) (Purkayastha et al., 2019). Type 2 conflicts were even worse when family ownership control was accompanied by family management control. Separating family ownership from family management helped firms to moderate Type 2 agency conflicts and keep Type 1 agency conflicts under control. However, Purkayastha and colleagues (2022) proposed that the most effective governance structure to reduce negative effects of both Type 1 and Type 2 agency conflicts is a family-controlled and non-family-managed firm. Many family firms would not be willing or find it practical to adopt this structure due to size and other factors, but the differences in control and in firm management present another potential for heterogeneous outcomes in the study of family business dysfunction.

5.3 Firm Reputation

A court in Antwerp, Belgium, convicted Alain and Sylvain Goetz, heirs to the refining and precious metals organization Tony Goetz NV and the family's numerous other commercial holdings, guilty of engaging in illegal trading activities that amounted to operating a black market for gold in 2020. Between 2010 and 2011, the brothers operated a fraudulent operation that comprised buying gold from unidentified consumers to avoid cash transaction limitations. Some of the company's gold purchases were suspected to be stolen as well. The plan netted Tony Goetz NV over $10 million. Alain and Sylvain Goetz received suspended sentences for their roles in the company's illegal activities, and Tony Goetz NV received a fine of almost $3 million from the authorities. As soon as the incident occurred, Tony Goetz NV changed its name to Industrial Refining Corporation. (SAI, 2023)

The reputation of an organization is based on outsider perceptions, including a combination of the assumptions and information that stakeholders can obtain about the business (Brown et al., 2006; Dyer & Whetten, 2006). Stakeholders develop varied views of the firm's reputation based on what they believe they know about the business and the family. The family firm's reputation is often associated with the family who owns it because the name of the owners is often the name of the company. Strong identification of family members with the firm can impact performance; the reverse can be true as well. Thus, as seen in the opening vignette to this subsection, firm names may be changed to divert attention and preserve reputation.

A family firm's reputation is extremely important due to the long-term legacy that the business seeks as it takes the family firm across generations. If family members are stained by engaging in bad behavior even unrelated to the work of the firm, the stain may easily spread to the business. In advancing a typology of family firm scandals that can tarnish firm reputation, Rondi et al. (2023) identified this type as a "black sheep" scandal. The authors used the example of François-Henri Pinault of a French fashion family business, who was publicly accused by former supermodel Linda Evangelista of failing to pay child support for a son he had not recognized as his own until the child was 5 years old. Again, the name of the company was eventually changed from PPR (Pinault-Printemps-Redoute) to Kering, thus separating the persona of the family member from that of the family firm.

The effects of dysfunctional behavior on the family firm's reputation may vary depending on several factors that were found in a recent meta-analysis to influence reputation including family involvement and control, firm characteristics, social ties, identification with the firm, and ethical values (Sageder et al., 2018). In other words, the degree to which the family firm is found to be consistent in its actions compared to its words will put it in a better position to weather the impact of dysfunction on its image and reputation. Two relevant contingencies would be the level of reputation versus the severity of the transgression, but some scandals such as the Adelphia fraud just cannot be overcome. In the Adelphia case, both the firm and its reputation were destroyed by the dysfunctional behavior of its leadership. A third contingency is that a family firm's response to wrongdoing may depend on whether the risk associated with the wrongdoing is destructive or productive considering the firm's economic and non-economic goals (Smulowitz et al., 2023).

5.4 Business Family Relationships

The impact of dysfunctional behavior is not only felt in the family business but also in the business family. Sadly, this seems appropriate considering the role that family relationships may have played as antecedents to bad behavior in the first place. When a family member engages in negative acts that hurt the firm as well as other individuals who work there, or other family members who do not, it not only creates future issues for the business, but also impacts the family (Eddleston & Kidwell, 2012). A family firm leader who has behaved lovingly and altruistically to an undeserving family member employee may have an unexpected reaction to the family member's negative work behavior: providing even more resources due to the leader's own feelings of guilt, particularly if the leader is the offender's parent. However, well-intentioned the leader is, this action may lead the Fredo—as he was called in Chapter 3 (or Freida because it should not be implied that these violators are all male)—to continue bad behavior and even escalate it.

These deviant and dysfunctional actions potentially create more emotional trauma for the family as relationships are strained. They are unique to family firms due to the overlap of business and family and the difficulty of separating work roles and family roles. A vicious circle of bad behavior can be inspired if the family firm leader continues to allow Fredo to continue in the firm. More bad behavior is rewarded by more altruistic behavior by the leader. This hits the firm and the family both financially and emotionally. Even if the leader takes a stern approach and eventually removes a Fredo from the firm, guilt may continue, and more emotional (and potentially financial) payments are made to preserve Fredo's place in family life. Yet, the tensions at holiday celebrations and family gatherings are palpable, at least for the leader, as the offender is not seen as such by other family members who are not engaged in the business and do not understand what happened.

In rare cases, the bad behavior destroys the family as well as its victims. In the Bernie Madoff case, in which the father defrauded investors of $65 billion and was reported by his sons to the FBI when they found out, the consequences were particularly tragic for the investors as well as the family. Not only was Madoff convicted and sentenced to 150 years in prison where he died in 2021, his whistleblowing sons, who worked in the legitimate arm of the company, predeceased him. Mark was found dead by suicide on the second anniversary of his father's arrest and Andrew died of cancer in 2014. Bernie Madoff's brother, Peter, who was also involved in the scheme, received a 10-year prison sentence (History.com Editors, 2011; Langer, 2014).

5.5 Constructive Deviance

Turning away from the negative outcomes of dysfunction, which have been emphasized thus far, provides an opportunity to frame deviance in family firms in a different way. Outcomes can be positive (Kidwell et al., 2019). It truly depends on the nature of the norms being broken that determines instances of positive, or constructive, deviance, another instance in which heterogeneity in family firms is observed. Some norms that might be found in a very few family firms are not considered acceptable at a societal level, such as fraud, corruption, and bribery (Warren, 2003). But there may be some norms that are held by family firms that could improve the business's performance if the key actors decided to break them. Such actions may be deviant from the established norms within the family firm, but they can bring positive outcomes to the family and the family business (Kidwell et al., 2019; Kim & Markus, 1999; Vadera et al., 2013).

Positive deviance has become an often-researched topic both as a theoretical concept and a practical strategy to identify and promote high performance in a wide spectrum of disciplines extending well beyond the family firm (Herington & van de Fliert, 2018: 674): "A continued emphasis on the negative aspects of deviance undermines an opportunity to explore … the important contribution that positive deviance in theory may produce in understanding the nature of modern society in the twenty-first century." When applied to family firms as a constructive mechanism, consideration generally starts with the family system where both positive and negative norms with differential results are established. In some family systems,

> (T)he elders set norms that provide for higher levels of creativity and constructive activity whereas in other systems a focus on tradition and stability may dominate and preclude creativity or challenges to the status quo and thus set the stage for creativity, innovation and change to be viewed as deviant. The value of what has worked in past and current generations may restrict positive views toward experimentation and challenge, but the intergenerational interplay between these two points of view is a key factor. (Kidwell et al., 2019: 658–659).

For example, it is the norm in some family firms for the founding generation to resist changing the ways of accomplishing goals as well as the content of the business models, objectives, and strategies to attain them. Creators and innovators of Generation 2 break this norm, and their deviance may turn out to be positive for the family, the firm and its stakeholders as unique products, novel services, and untapped markets are discovered. In other firms, paternalism and primogeniture may be the norm. Female leaders and others who challenge the status quo may break this norm, but their deviant behavior may take the firm in a new and positive direction. Some family firm members or non-family employees may be faced with a norm of silence in terms of questioning the actions of family firm leaders. Those exercising voice or whistleblowing when there is wrongdoing are deviating from the norm, but the company may experience a positive result even if it hurts the leaders who are strongly invested in preserving the firm's norms and the rules and policies that are there to enforce them.

5.6 Strategic Deviance/Dysfunction

> Almost from the beginning, Crazy Eddie engaged in fraudulent business practices, including under-reporting income, skimming sales taxes, and paying employees off the books. These practices, in conjunction with aggressive sales tactics, enabled Crazy Eddie to significantly undercut competitors and grow rapidly. During the process of going public, Crazy Eddie continued to engage in fraud, over-reporting profits, inflating inventory, and duping auditors. Unable to sustain his fraudulent business practices, co-founder Eddie Antar cashed in millions of dollars' worth of stock and resigned from the company in December 1986. Crazy Eddie's board of directors approved the sale of the company in November 1987. The entire Antar family was immediately removed from the business. The new owners quickly discovered the true extent of the Antar family's fraud but were unable to turn around Crazy Eddie's quickly declining fortunes. In 1989, the company filed for bankruptcy and was liquidated. (Wikipedia.org, 2023)

Whether deviant behavior is constructive or destructive, functional or dysfunctional, the business family and the family business may strategically engage in it (Kidwell et al., 2019). Strategic deviance is defined as "the complementary use of organizational mechanisms and actions that may violate established norms and be perceived as dysfunctional yet contribute to overall system wellbeing. Strategic deviance provides a rationale as to why apparently negative behaviors are accepted and potentially take on an ambiguous character" (Kidwell & Nygaard, 2011: 468). This ambiguity relates to the idea that businesses will strategically establish governance practices that deviate from established norms depending on the regulatory environment and other factors (Aguilera et al., 2018).

The family owners of Crazy Eddie needed no such contingencies to form a deliberate company strategy of fraudulent business practices to operate their electronics store chain in New York through the 1970s and 1980s. They engaged in dysfunctional and deviant behavior as part of an intentional business model. Despite the negative example of "Crazy Eddie" Antar, those family members who raise major issues that are traditionally not discussed or debated to assist in guiding the business are engaging in a form of strategic deviance that could ultimately benefit the organization. A more positive model involves a new generation that leads a family firm to engage in a strategic culture change by replacing antiquated values such as an emphasis on stability toward an emphasis on flexibility when environmental conditions dictate that such a deviation from the norm is needed.

Earlier, the practice of nepotism and its potentially positive outcomes for family firm stewardship were discussed. In some societies and cultures, nepotism policies are considered the norm while in others an owner hiring family members over more qualified non-family job applicants is seen as violating a norm, workplace discrimination being generally viewed unfavorably by many societies (Jaskiewicz et al., 2013). Whereas societal norms may see nepotism as deviant and detrimental, many family businesses may benefit at the firm level by hiring and appointing family members. These firms wish to have a workforce that shares similar values and allows the firm's future leaders to gain important skills (Salvato et al., 2012) or to enhance family control by appointing family members to director positions on company boards in effect engaging in strategic nepotism (Jeong et al., 2022). However, if the firm is discriminating against non-family applicants by hiring or appointing *less qualified* family members, the family's potential deviance from a societal-level norm may be seen as dysfunctional rather than strategic.

Finally, family leaders may use strategic deviance unethically by treating their Fredo, the "problem child" in the family business, in a way that helps control the actions of other family members (Kidwell et al., 2019). Making a black sheep such as Fredo into a scapegoat, a form of bullying in which Fredo is assigned blame for anything that goes wrong, is deviant and dysfunctional yet not unusual. Treatment of the scapegoat can be used to get other family members to comply, or face being targeted as the next victim. Such dysfunctional (and probably unethical) use of deviance could be employed strategically as discipline to maintain stability and continuity by both the family and family firm leaders, but its use has the potential to damage the long-term health of the business family and the family business.

5.7 Concluding Comments

Considering the outcomes of dysfunctional behavior on individuals, business families, family businesses, and stakeholders (customers, competitors, regulators, community members, and government to name a few), we see the heterogeneous nature of dysfunction and deviance in family firms.

Both negative and positive outcomes of dysfunction and deviance can be observed, some of them short term and some of them long term, some minor and others with the strength to take down the company. The idea that deviance can be positive and constructive depending on the nature of the deviance and the nature of the norms being broken contrasts with the positives that may be found with dysfunction. Dysfunctional behaviors' true positives (for individuals, families, and firms) only come at the expense of the targets. This provides an important distinction between dysfunction and deviance.

The next chapter details additional antecedents of dysfunction and deviant behavior that may arise from early childhood and other family interactions as well as the environment's impact on the functioning of family firms. These proposed antecedents stem from several different theories related to families and to family firms. The theoretical perspectives provide additional ways to frame future research and to assist families, family firms, and their advisors in making sense of dysfunction across families and family firms and help address the question of why some family firms are dysfunctional and others are not.

References

Aguilera, R. V., Judge, W. Q., & Terjesen, S. A. (2018). Corporate governance deviance. *Academy of Management Review, 43*(1), 87–109.

Ahrens, J. P., Landmann, A., & Woywode, M. (2015). Gender preferences in the CEO successions of family firms: Family characteristics and human capital of the successor. *Journal of Family Business Strategy, 6*(2), 86–103.

Ahrens, J. P., Uhlaner, L., Woywode, M., & Zybura, J. (2018). "Shadow emperor" or "loyal paladin"?—The Janus face of previous owner involvement in family firm successions. *Journal of Family Business Strategy, 9*(1), 73–90.

Beauge, J. (2023, June 6). Court supervision ends for last Rigas family member in Adelphia fraud scandal, https://www.pennlive.com/news/2023/06/court-supervision-ends-for-last-rigas-family-member-in-adelphia-fraud-scandal.html. Accessed December 1, 2023.

Blanco-Mazagatos, V., Quevedo-Puente, E., & Delgado-Garcia, J. (2016). How agency conflict between family managers and family owners affects performance in wholly family-owned firms: A generational perspective. *Journal of Family Business Strategy, 7*, 167–177.

Brown, T. J., Dacin, P. A., Pratt, M. G., & Whetten, D. A. (2006). Identity, intended image, construed image, and reputation: An interdisciplinary framework and suggested terminology. *Journal of the Academy of Marketing Science, 34*(2), 99–106.

Bull, G. (2004, July 8). *Adelphia founder John Rigas found guilty*. NBC News. https://www.nbcnews.com/id/wbna5396406. Accessed October 20, 2023.

Cater, J. J., III., & Kidwell, R. E. (2014). Function, governance, and trust in successor leadership groups in family firms. *Journal of Family Business Strategy, 5*(3), 217–228.

Cater, J. J., III., Kidwell, R. E., & Camp, K. M. (2016). Successor team dynamics in family firms. *Family Business Review, 29*(3), 301–326.

Dyer, W. G., Jr., & Whetten, D. A. (2006). Family firms and social responsibility: Preliminary evidence from the S&P 500. *Entrepreneurship Theory and Practice, 30*(6), 785–802.

Eddleston, K.A., & Kidwell, R E. (2012). Parent–child relationships: Planting the seeds of deviant behavior in the family firm. *Entrepreneurship Theory and Practice, 36*(2), 369–386

Handler, W. C. (1991). Key interpersonal relationships of next-generation family members in family firms. *Journal of Small Business Management, 29*(3), 21.

Herington, M. J., & van de Fliert, E. (2018). Positive deviance in theory and practice: A conceptual review. *Deviant Behavior, 39*(5), 664–678.

History.com Editors. (2011, July 20). *This day in history December 11, 2008, Billionaire con man Bernie Madoff arrested*. https://www.history.com/this-day-in-history/billionaire-conman-bernard-madoff-arrested. Accessed October 20, 2023.

Hoelscher, M. (2014). Does family capital outweigh the negative effects of conflict on firm performance? *Journal of Family Business Management, 4*(1), 46–61.

Hudson, S., González-Gómez, H. V., & Claasen, C. (2019). Legitimacy, particularism and employee commitment and justice. *Journal of Business Ethics, 157*(3), 589–603.

Jain, S. S., Fernando, G. D., Tripathy, A., & Bhatia, S. (2021). Closing the gender gap in top management teams: An examination of diversity and compensation parity in family and non-family firms. *Journal of Family Business Strategy, 12*(4), https://doi.org/10.1016/j.jfbs.2020.100388

Jaskiewicz, P., Uhlenbruck, K., Balkin, D. B., & Reay, T. (2013). Is nepotism good or bad? Types of nepotism and implications for knowledge management. *Family Business Review, 26*(2), 121–139.

Jennings, J., Dempsey, D., & James, A. (2018). Bifurcated HR practices in family firms: Insights from the normative-adaptive approach to stepfamilies. *Human Resource Management Review, 28*(1), 68–82.

Jeong, S. H., Kim, H., & Kim, H. (2022). Strategic nepotism in family director appointments: Evidence from family business groups in South Korea. *Academy of Management Journal, 65*(2), 656–682.

Kidwell, R. E., Cox, K. C., & Kloepfer, K. E. (2019). The diversity of deviance: How it can hurt (and help) families and family firms. In *The Palgrave handbook of heterogeneity among family firms* (pp. 643–672). Springer.

Kidwell, R. E., Eddleston, K. A., Cater, J. J., & Kellermanns, F. W. (2013). How one bad family member can undermine a family firm: Preventing the Fredo effect. *Business Horizons, 56*(1), 5–12.

Kidwell, R. E., & Nygaard, A. (2011). A strategic deviance perspective on the franchise form of organizing. *Entrepreneurship Theory & Practice, 35*(3), 467–482.

Kim, H., & Markus, H. R. (1999). Deviance or uniqueness, harmony, or conformity? A cultural analysis. *Journal of Personality and Social Psychology, 77*, 785–800.

Langer, E. (2014). Andrew F. Madoff, son of convicted financier, dies at 48. *The Washington Post*. https://www.washingtonpost.com/national/andrew-h-madoff-son-of-convicted-financier-dies-at-48/2014/09/03/49c10da4-0e81-11e4-b8e5-d0de80767fc2_story.html. Accessed October 20, 2023.

Minichilli, A., Corbetta, G., & MacMillan, I. C. (2010). Top management teams in family-controlled companies: 'Familiness,' 'faultlines,' and their impact on financial performance. *Journal of Management Studies, 47*(2), 205–222.

Overbeke, K. K., Bilimoria, D., & Perelli, S. (2013). The dearth of daughter successors in family businesses: Gendered norms, blindness to possibility, and invisibility. *Journal of Family Business Strategy, 4*(3), 201–212.

Purkayastha, S., Veliyath, R., & George, R. (2019). The roles of family ownership and family management in the governance of agency conflicts. *Journal of Business Research, 98*, 50–64.

Purkayastha, S., Veliyath, R., & George, R. (2022). Type I and type II agency conflicts in family firms: An empirical investigation. *Journal of Business Research, 153*, 285–299.

Rondi, E., Benedetti, C., Bettinelli, C., & De Massis, A. (2023). Falling from grace: Family based brands amidst scandals. *Journal of Business Research, 157*, 113637.

Sacristan-Navarro, M., & Cabeza-Garcia, L. (2019). When family firm corporate governance fails: The case of El Corte Ingles. *Journal of Family Business Management, 10*(2), 97–115.

Sageder, M., Mitter, C., & Feldbauer-Durstmüller, B. (2018). Image and reputation of family firms: A systematic literature review of the state of research. *Review of Managerial Science, 12*, 335–377.

SAI. (2023). *10 Family business scandals that caused chaos*. Medium https://medium.com/@imsaisuman/10-family-business-scandals-that-caused-chaos-5d38cc3ce372. Accessed October 12, 2023.

Salvato, C., Minichilli, A., & Piccarreta, R. (2012). Faster route to the CEO suite: Nepotism or managerial proficiency? *Family Business Review, 25*(2), 206–224.

Schmid, A., & Sender, A. (2021). How social capital influences performance in family firms: The moderating role of nepotism. *The International Journal of Human Resource Management, 32*(18), 3973–3993.

Smulowitz, S. J., Cossin, D., De Massis, A., & Lu, H. (2023). Wrongdoing in publicly listed family-and nonfamily-owned firms: A behavioral perspective. *Entrepreneurship Theory and Practice, 47*(4), 1233–1264.

Sylvers, E. (2019). Parmalat vs. Citigroup: 15 years after Italian scandal, court fight rages on. *Wall Street Journal*. https://www.wsj.com/articles/citigroup-loses-a-round-in-its-15-year-pursuit-of-funds-from-parmalat-11553688295. Accessed October 10, 2023.

Vadera, A. K., Pratt, M. G., & Mishra, P. (2013). Constructive deviance in organizations: Integrating and moving forward. *Journal of Management, 39*, 1221–1276.

Warren, D. E. (2003). Constructive and destructive deviance in organizations. *Academy of Management Review, 29*, 622–632.

Wikipedia.Org. (2023). *Crazy Eddie*. https://en.wikipedia.org/wiki/Crazy_Eddie#cite_note-frankensteins-3. Accessed October 15, 2023.

CHAPTER 6

Fertile Ground for Exploring the Roots of "Bad" Behavior

Abstract After summarizing the various theories employed in the study of family business dysfunction, this chapter returns focus to the family system to encourage the study of how several theories developed in the family studies arena can aid explanation and prediction of why and when deviance and dysfunction occur in some family firms. Changing definitions of family, the establishment and growth of the family as well as theories such as family systems, parental control, family niche-model of birth order and personality, family communication patterns, developmental psychology, and kinship theory can tell more about the roots of bad behavior than has been revealed thus far. The firm's external context is also examined to determine the roles that national culture and potentially race and ethnicity play in how bad behavior is viewed and managed in diverse family firms.

Keywords Dysfunctional families · Social exchange theory · Family systems theory · Parenting styles · Family communication patterns · Kinship ties · Cultural differences · Family firms

> "My sister has a marketing agency, and she helps clients do social media marketing, and brand positioning. And my mom did hire her services and

R. E. Kidwell, *Dysfunction and Deviance Across Family Firms*, Palgrave Studies in Family Business Heterogeneity,
https://doi.org/10.1007/978-3-031-51816-4_6

that was also part of a little conflict because she didn't even tell me about it. My sister and I don't have the best relationship and.... from the beginning my mom's desire was to have both her daughters grow this business with her. But the reality is that she needed to choose me or her because we just didn't get along, and obviously my mom knew. My sister has never been the one daughter that sacrificed stuff for her. I was that daughter. I will put up my credit.'You need a card? No problem, I'll cosign for you.' 'Do you need me to put up my credit so we can be approved for an American Express credit card? No problem, I'll do that for us.' Whereas my sister was more like: what's in it for me? I'm not going to sacrifice me for this.'"—Former family business owner discussing parent and sibling relationships in the now-defunct family firm that she started with her mother (Interviewed by author, March 2021).

"I guess for us it's always just been equality, but more than anything, integrity, for us, has been the biggest thing. This industry is ripe for corruption. There're so many opportunities to do crooked things. You know, put a little extra cash in your pocket by hiring this guy or put money in somebody else's pocket to get the job. And we've been very fortunate that we've been able to stay above board with all that stuff. and you have to if you want your company to have longevity and maintain its highest status or stature in the industry, you got to do it."—Family firm member and chief operating officer of a $65 million construction company (Interviewed by author, June 2021).

In addition to the causes, content, and impact of dysfunctional and deviant behavior in family firms, two other key questions from the introductory chapter need to be addressed. The first is to further examine what factors might make it more or less likely for either family or non-family employees to engage in dysfunctional behavior directed at the family, the family firm, or the external stakeholders. The second is to provide a general review of theoretical perspectives and previous research that might influence future research on the heterogeneity of dysfunction and deviance in the family firm. These questions will be addressed in Chapter 6 with a specific focus on theories that are currently driving studies of families and family systems. Chapter 7 will expand on future research directions and describe a theoretical framework that can guide future research into differences within and across family firms on the topic of dysfunction in the family business.

One theme of this chapter is a return to the consideration of family processes, family structure, and early family relationships in attempting to identify factors that differentially connect family relationships with dysfunctional behavior in a way that moderates the impact of antecedents on negative behaviors. The second theme is to look outside the firm to see if there are additional factors in the external environment that may explain why some family firms engage in negative behaviors and others do not. This chapter considers what happens to family members before they enter the family firm and what happens in the external environment that could have an impact on the behaviors of family firm leaders as well as family and non-family employees. First, theoretical perspectives that have guided research in the topic thus far are important to briefly review.

6.1 Theoretical Perspectives

The study of deviance and dysfunction has incorporated a variety of theoretical perspectives that cross the disciplines of psychology, sociology, economics, accounting, and finance. When family firm research is considered across levels of analysis, a similar mixture of theorizing occurs—based generally on the discipline of the researchers and the focus of the research.

As noted earlier, social exchange theory—described as one of the broadest conceptual frameworks in organizational behavior research—has been used to describe and explain many behaviors involving two or more individuals (Cropanzano et al., 2017) and encompasses various acts that can be described as deviant and/or dysfunctional (Mackey et al., 2021). The social exchange model is loosely described as your beneficial (harmful) actions toward me engender a high-quality (low-quality) exchange relationship that informs my positive (negative) actions toward you (Cropanzano et al., 2017). The model has been used to explain family interactions that identify potential antecedents of negative behaviors between actors within the family and the family firm (e.g., Hudson et al., 2019; Jaskiewicz et al., 2013). These also include perceived justice or injustices that can lead to negative acts (e.g., Waterwall & Alipour, 2021; Zheng et al., 2017).

As would be expected, when studies of dysfunction's antecedents focus on interpersonal relationships and intragroup conflict, conflict theory is a major organizing principle (e.g., Haag & Achtenhagen, 2021; Islas-Moreno et al., 2021; Kellermanns & Eddleston, 2004; Rosecká & Machek, 2022). These studies focus on issues such as how divorce disrupts the family firm (e.g., Haag & Achtenhagen, 2021), how cognitive and interpersonal conflicts affect family firm performance (Kellermanns & Eddleston, 2004, 2007), and how conflict increases as family firms broaden to multiple generations and relationships become more distant (Davis & Harveston, 2001).

When the conflict is raised to the firm level and takes on the role of a dysfunctional behavior and not merely a precursor of negative actions, the theoretical perspectives shift to agency theory and stewardship theory (e.g., Blanco-Mazagatos et al., 2016; Purkayastha et al., 2019). These studies consider the impact of family ownership and management on opportunistic behavior (e.g., Schulze et al., 2001) and the effects of altruism and self-control problems on gains in agency costs resulting from family ownership (Xiang et al., 2014). Researchers incorporate social as well as organizational identity theory at various levels of analysis including the effects of personality on dysfunctional behavior (Galvin et al., 2015), bifurcation bias (Kim & Marler, 2020), corporate social irresponsibility (Cruz et al., 2014), and tax evasion (Eddleston & Mulki, 2021). In brief, social identity refers to an individual's knowledge that he/she belongs to certain groups such as "family member" or "nonfamily employee" and experiences the emotions and value attached to that membership whereas organizational identity refers to shared meanings that a family or family firm possess that derive from its members' awareness they belong to the family or the firm (cf., Cornelissen et al., 2007).

Stakeholder theory and institutional theory have also been employed to consider the family firm's performance regarding corporate social responsibility (Block & Wagner, 2014), extremes in treatment of external stakeholders (Miller & Le Breton-Miller, 2021), and negative environmental performance (Berrone et al., 2010; Kim et al., 2017). In general, institutional theory emphasizes pressures on the firm generated from formal institutions and other companies in the field in which it operates while stakeholder theory has a broader focus on the many and often conflicting demands made by the family firm's many different stakeholders (cf. Barrena-Martínez et al., 2016).

As noted in Chapter 2, a great deal of research into deviance and dysfunction has been guided by the concept of socioemotional wealth (SEW), less a theory than a concept that has formed an important basis of differentiation between family firms and non-family firms. SEW has been defined as "the non-financial aspects of the firm that meet the family's affective needs, such as identity, the ability to exercise family influence, and the perpetuity of the family dynasty" (Gomez-Mejia et al., 2007: 106). As SEW's focus is on the family as beneficiary when its pursuits bear fruit, non-tangible so they may be, it has been argued whether SEW involves merely self-interested behavior or something larger (Craig & Newbert, 2020; Miller & LeBreton-Miller, 2014; Newbert & Craig, 2017). The varied motivations of the family in how, why, and to what lengths SEW is pursued by the family firm lead to further consideration of how families and family relationships and systems develop over time—sometimes resulting in dysfunctional families that have the potential for strong impact on what the family firm has—or will—become.

6.2 Dysfunctional Families—A Shock to the System

> This was a family where the parenting regime was harsh – authoritarian rather than authoritative in the jargon of family theory. Fred (Koch) Sr had the frontier spirit, and had become an entrepreneurial dragon, forging his way forward through calculated risk taking and a succession of legal and business battles with Big Oil. His four sons were brought up under a strict disciplinarian regime and were expected to work for the firm through their holidays and at all times to live up to the very highest standards of behavior. The eldest son, Frederick, like Cain, earned his father's extreme disfavor over an alleged act that the father strongly disapproved of. Despite Frederick's strenuous protestations of innocence, Fred Sr., like a vengeful deity, concluded that he wished to sever all connections with his son, transferring his bequest on to his other offspring. The second son, Charles, was the most ambitious, driven and hardworking, like his father. As a youngster he pushed his brothers around when they played a game they knew as 'King of the Hill'. The youngest two brothers, David and William (Billy), were twins. Of the two, Billy was the forceful character, and bridled at the tough treatment he received from his dad, as well as the bullying he received from his older brother Charles.—Koch family case (Gordon & Nicholson, 2008; excerpt from Kidwell et al., 2018: 8).

Early family relationships as antecedents to dysfunctional behavior were discussed briefly in Chapter 2. Here these relationships—parents and children, sisters and brothers, and other kinship connections—are revisited and placed in the context of the family system. Family business research into the connections between such topics as early conflict in the family and later dysfunction in the family firm may benefit from considering the work of colleagues in family studies (Kidwell et al., 2023). Different theoretical and conceptual approaches taken by researchers in family therapy, family psychology, and family communications can be applied from the workings of the family to their impact on the family firm. Once again, dysfunction and deviance have varied opportunities to arise across family firms based on a variety of factors dating from the origin, interactions, and growth (or lack thereof) of the family or families involved. Two questions to consider are (1) to what extent do dysfunctional families breed dysfunctional family firms? and (2) to what extent do dysfunctional family firms increase the dysfunction in families?

The circular nature of the questions indicates the impact that the family system has on individuals within it as well as on the associated family firm—and conversely the impact that the business system has on the family and its members. Family systems theory (Bowen, 1978; Broderick, 1993; Olson, 2000) focuses on the interdependent and complex nature of the family, not only in how parents affect children, but how children affect parents, and siblings impact each other and other family members, all as part of an open social system. The family system is a setting for development of processes that establish and develop rules, role characteristics, power structure, and communication patterns that extend beyond the individual members. If these processes are executed properly, they have a greater relationship with a family business being sustainable than do the firm's personalities and structural design (Zachary et al., 2023). However, if they are not tended to properly, the conditions for dysfunction in the family firm become apparent.

A central premise of Bowen's family systems theory is that individuals may be more understood based on the context of their family relationships. Thus, the opening vignette about the Koch family is less about the father and more about relationships that the family shaped based on their interactions and how these influenced the subsequent functioning of the family and eventually the business. While the father is portrayed as an authoritarian putting a great deal of negative pressure on his children, the systems view would see reciprocal and lateral familial relationships resulting in levels of dysfunction that would differentiate one family from another.

Dysfunctional family systems have long been the topic of research in the family science field (e.g., Conger, 1981). Yet, with some exceptions (e.g., Haag & Achtenhagen, 2021; Shanine et al., 2023), they have received relatively little study in the realm of family business. This is so even though the seeds of dysfunction that blossom, so to speak, in the firm are planted in the family (poor parent–child relationships, negative sibling dynamics, poor communication) and then reinforced through continued interactions that make for a vicious circle of behaviors that develop into dysfunctional family members and/or a dysfunctional family system. As a result, dysfunctional families are wrought with tumultuous relationships that end in the downfall of some families (Constantine, 1983). Even so, the deleterious effects of dysfunctional elements such as conflict within the family vary across family firms, and the stresses they create can be weathered by many of them (Kubíček & Machek, 2020; Qiu & Freel, 2020).

6.3 Parental Impact on Child Development

Whereas family systems theory provides a more holistic view of the development and functioning of family relationships, the ingredients for the system also produce differences in dysfunctional behavior across family firms. These are engendered by the quality of parent–child relationships, the nature of sibling dynamics and peer relationships, and the quality of communication within the family. The next sections examine each of these, identifying relevant family science theories and applying studies conducted in family psychology, family therapy, developmental psychology, and communication studies. The findings suggest how the effects of relationships, dynamics, and communication may vary across families and family firms.

The effects of childhood roles (scapegoat, hero) and parenting styles (authoritarian, permissive, authoritative) were suggested as antecedents of dysfunctional behaviors in Chapter 2. One major family science perspective discussed in Chapter 2 was parental control theory in which parenting styles were linked to subsequent behavior of the children when they become adults. An authoritative style was regarded as a more positive approach while authoritarian and permissive styles were seen as having potentially negative effects. Effects of the parenting style can turn up when the children are grown and working in the family firm, and this can impact their family member employees and potential successors.

In some cases, authoritarian parents violate a perceived boundary between home and work by continuing to direct their children even though they are now adult employees and often business executives in the firm (Kidwell et al., 2019). This action may threaten the child's identity as a "grownup" and cause a revolt. Indeed, the founder's parenting style affects a successor's psychological functioning, which can have positive (organizational citizenship behavior) and/or negative (counterproductive behavior) results (Shanine et al., 2023).

In addition, while parents may model behaviors that have the potential for positive effects for their children, they may also model negative behaviors that have been connected to anxiety and destructive behavior in children (e.g., Fisak & Grills-Taquechel, 2007). Parental behavior and parental values help set norms that evolve into a shared family culture that has the potential for varied results depending on the nature of the norms that are perpetuated, for example, norms of interparental cooperation versus interparental conflict (Davies et al., 2019). Just as a founder establishes values and norms in a new venture that become the company culture, parents establish norms within the family that potentially endure across generations such as respect for authority, strength of social bonds, and effective communication styles. Yet, negative norms can also be perpetuated by the parents such as disrespect for authority, interpersonal conflict, and poor communication. These examples can be transmitted to the next generation (Simons et al., 1991) raising perceptions of injustice in how parents treat adolescent and adult siblings (Jensen et al., 2013; Loeser et al., 2016). Thus, the potential for heterogeneity in the effects of parenting style on subsequent dysfunction and deviance across family firms seems apparent.

Another lens in which to view parents' (and others') influence on children and their subsequent actions as adults, for better and for worse, is developmental psychology (Kidwell et al., 2023). Developmental psychology examines an individual's progress, growth, and change over time and is studied in stages such as psychosocial development, adulthood development (e.g., Levinson, 1978), and identity crisis /role confusion (e.g., Erikson, 1963; Maree, 2021). Applied to the family and the firm, developmental psychology may help explain the heterogeneity of deviance and dysfunction (antecedents in particular) by examining how family members grow emotionally, intellectually, and socially before joining the family firm and how they adapt to change during that process. It may be possible to better understand how family members cope with conflict in the family firm by recognizing that family members and peers are involved in most of the conflict a person experiences as a child and an adolescent (Laursen & Pursell, 2009). Both childhood experiences and parental behaviors that clash with an individual's expectations and beliefs can lead to serious issues arising later in that person's work experience (Müller et al., 2022.)

6.4 Siblings' (and Peers') Effects on Children and Adults

Siblings form the longest-lasting relationships in most people lives (Gilligan et al., 2020), and cooperation (or rivalry) between them is particularly important to the success (or failure) of many family firms. The impact of sibling rivalry on deviant and dysfunctional behavior was briefly discussed in Chapter 2. The lack of ability for siblings to get along with one another, or speak to one another, can date from childhood experiences, but it can have impact on family firms after the siblings become adults. For example, in the succession process, satisfaction with the process was found to be lower when sibling conflict is present (Handler, 1991). In addition, conflicts, especially between siblings, erode family harmony and endanger the firm's survival (Jayantilal et al., 2016). Sibling dynamics can be affected by parental divorce and their perceptions of their parents' marital satisfaction (Milevsky, 2019), and they can become estranged from each other as adults (Blake et al., 2022). All these factors have high potential to affect some family firms but not others as do cooperative, synergistic, and loving relationships among siblings.

Social exchange is a key theoretical basis "for investigating sibling relationships along with theories of family systems and life course perspectives to gain a better understanding of the structure, function, processes, and meaning of sibling relationships in middle and later life" (Gilligan et al., 2020: 305). In addition, the family-niche-model of birth order and personality is useful in examining relations with parents and siblings as it proposes that a child's personality development is influenced by the way siblings create niches based on birth order to gain access to their parents' resources (Sulloway, 1996). The view that "first borns are reported to be more responsible and achievement oriented than later borns, who are in turn reported to be more socially successful than older siblings" (Sulloway, 1996: 55) has implications for sibling relationships in addition to parental influence. Sulloway (1996) proposed that to obtain parental resources first-born children try to please their parents by being successful and responsible and by developing into conscientious adults whereas later-born children develop an empathic adult character that strives for uniqueness that can result in rebellion (Paulhus et al., 1999).

The model has differential outcomes that have implications for the siblings when they join the family firm in that an intense sibling competition may result in development of creativity on the part of some children and in development of the Dark Triad of personality traits (Machiavellianism, narcissism, and psychopathy) among others (Paulhus & Williams, 2002). This theory may help explain another source of the differential impact of dysfunction in the family firm. It lends support to the concept of virtuous and vicious circles of behavior developing among siblings in family firms (Eddleston & Kidwell, 2012).

In addition, developmental psychology approaches can provide insights for family firm research into how dysfunctional behavior such as bullying—potentially led by an older brother who victimizes his younger siblings (Menesini et al., 2010)—develops and changes over time. Research indicates that insensitive parenting, coercive interaction, family instability, and family dysfunction help explain the development of bullying within a family (Rodkin et al., 2015). When children experience coercive relationships at home and are exposed to violence in the family, they may expect that a basic element of all interpersonal relationships is aggression and that affects their expectations and guides their behavior when they interact with others (Rodkin, et al., 2015). Peer influence is another important factor that affects attitudes and behaviors that can be positive or negative (Laursen & Veenstra, 2021; Yoho et al., 2022), Thus, siblings may bully each other as well as their peers, and this behavior can continue into adulthood—and the family business. Yet, once the younger victims have grown up and joined the family firm, they may be in a position that enables them to fight back economically rather than physically.

6.5 Kinship Ties, Dysfunction, and Function

Another perspective that is receiving recent attention in attempting to explain heterogeneity in family firms is evolutionary psychology, which presents insights into genetic factors that might lead to such behaviors as altruism or conflict (Madison et al., 2021; Nicholson, 2008; O'Brien et al., 2018). Applying Darwin's theory of natural selection to families and family firms, the evolutionary perspective stresses the concept of kinship in which individuals who share another person's genes are hardwired to help them, and their assistance will help spread that person's genes into future generations (O'Brien et al., 2018)—often disregarding any negative impact it may cause to distant kin or non-family members. An evolutionary perspective has been employed to study behavior across family firms in such areas as executive compensation (Yu et al., 2020), theft (O'Brien et al., 2018), preferential benefits (Stewart, 2020), and citizenship behavior (Madison et al., 2021).

When family members focus on assisting relatives in hiring and promotion, they may be surfacing kinship ties that provide the groundwork for nepotism and an increased potential for bifurcation bias. Further exploration of kinship ties as they relate to other factors within the family firm such as altruism can help explain what drives the antecedents of dysfunctional behavior and what the consequences of those negative behaviors are for business families and family businesses (Kidwell et al., 2023). For example, multigeneration firms may have developed more distant kinship ties (cousin consortia in the third generation), which could make it less difficult to put policies in place against dysfunctional nepotism to reduce the level of bias experienced by non-family employees.

Research results in family business studies using the evolutionary psychology/kinship perspective suggest that families and family firms have a more conscious strategy to manage nepotism (Collin & Ahlberg, 2012), that closeness of kinship ties and family membership is related to nepotism perceptions and are important to understanding the experiences and attitudes of employees in family firms (Spranger et al., 2012), and that kinship ties in new firms can have heterogeneous effects on performance depending on how they are structured (Ertug et al., 2020).

6.6 Communication: The Family and the Firm

Family Communication Patterns Theory (FCPT) is also relevant to the study of family influences on deviant and dysfunctional behavior in the family firm and the potential for differential behaviors and outcomes. FCPT is a general theory of family communication focusing on parent–child communication that is concerned with establishing a shared social reality (Koerner et al., 2017). The theory identifies basic processes resulting in a shared agreement that impacts not only short-term communication, but long-term information processing, psychosocial, and behavioral outcomes. FCPT claims to describe what family communication is and how it functions; it is not ideological, interpretive, or critical. The theory uses the dimensions of conversation and conformity to understand the degree of effective communication in families, and the influence of family patterns of agreement and disagreement on communication norms defining the family (Ritchie & Fitzpatrick, 1990) and describes the degree to which effective communication occurs in families. Family communication patterns learned throughout childhood have far reaching consequences into adulthood (Koerner & Fitzpatrick, 2002) and may influence how family firms operate.

In families with a high conversational orientation, family members are encouraged to discuss any topic of interest whereas when a high conformity orientation is present, family members emphasize accepting similar attitudes, values, and beliefs (Fitzpatrick & Ritchie, 1994). Such orientations reflect the level of normative conformity in the family and how those who deviate from norms are treated and the degree to which discussion of the effectiveness and appropriateness of current norms can take place. Although research is limited, both dimensions can affect the level and nature of deviant behavior in the family and the family firm.

For example, one study of family farm members who must balance family relationships and business concerns, which can cause conflict among members, indicated that respondents struggled with communication (Paskewitz & Beck, 2017). This struggle influenced family conflict over status within the firm as well as an individual's communication satisfaction. Another study involving parent–child entrepreneurs had more positive results: Children of entrepreneurs formed a positive entrepreneurial attitude if they believed their parents are passionate (Soleimanof et al., 2021). This effect was found to be strongest in families that adopt high levels of both conversation and conformity communication patterns.

Communication researchers also explore when situations go wrong in terms of communication between parents and adult children or among family members. Marginalization, alienation, and estrangement are all potential outcomes that can severely disrupt the family system (Scharp & Dorrance Hall, 2017). As little research exists regarding parent–child estrangement despite it being a widespread phenomenon (Scharp & Dorrance Hall, 2017; Scharp et al., 2015), this may be a worthwhile area of inquiry to extend to family firms seeking to understand various forms of dysfunctional behavior and their effects across family firms. In studies of alienation and estrangement, communication studies research emphasizes the communicative practices that are used by children to distance themselves from their parents (Scharp, 2019; Scharp et al., 2015), and the chronically stressful feelings of marginalization that result from hurtful communication (Dorrance Hall, 2017). Results from alienation need not always be negative in that conformity to a family's values, attitudes, and belief again depends on the nature of those norms. Thus, deviance from the norms might be seen in a positive light, particularly when the family itself has a great deal of dysfunction (Beck et al., 2011; Scharp & Dorrance Hall, 2017).

6.7 Deviance and Dysfunction across Cultures, Families, and Firms

Changing norms and values in the family's and the firm's external environment implies cultural shifts that affect the definition of family and the acceptance of some behaviors once thought deviant and dysfunctional (Kidwell et al., 2023). Examining dysfunction and deviance across cultures also leads to a diversity of views as to what behaviors are seen as negative and what behaviors are seen as the "normal" way of doing business for the family firm both internally, e.g., gender discrimination, and externally, e.g., bribery. This section addresses the effects of culture to potentially moderate the connection between antecedents of dysfunctional/deviant behavior, its occurrence, and its impact.

One important element to consider when connecting families to family firms is the changing perception of what constitutes a family (Zachary et al., 2023). The family or families operating a business could consist of couples who are heterosexual, homosexual, married, remarried, cohabiting with or without children, separated, or divorced—or single adults with children. When family systems are applied to family business (e.g., Combs et al., 2020), it is important to consider changing gender roles (Aldrich et al., 2021; Kushins & Behounek, 2020), varying role ideologies across generations (Gamboni et al., 2021), and the nuances presented by socio-legal, social-biological, and role-based families (Kushins & Behounek, 2020). As the definition of family evolves, the definition of the family firm and the implications for deviance and dysfunction will adjust as well.

Cultural or ethnic identity structures are also a consideration when examining business families and family firms. For example, in some large firms in India, extended families (brothers and sisters and their spouses and offspring as well as grandchildren) may live in a family compound located in the vicinity of the principal business or affiliated firms, which may imply different types and frequency of interactions among the many family members that impact the power of kinship ties. Differences in city, regional, or national norms, such as the importance of the family versus the firm in certain cultures (Zachary et al., 2023), are likely to affect how behaviors like nepotism and primogeniture are viewed. These differences, which have varied impacts across business families and their firms may be rooted in how the firm's systems develop in cultural and societal contexts, strongly affecting differences in types/ levels of dysfunctional behaviors and their effects (Kidwell et al., 2023). How dysfunction is identified and measured may be inaccurate when a disparity exists between the external environment and a family firm's cultural beliefs (Bamaca-Colbert et al., 2019). Therefore, to match the cultural context, researchers may need to adjust how they approach and define such elements as ethical behavior, corporate social irresponsibility, nepotism, and bribery (e.g., Samara et al., 2021).

Additional research in this domain would provide more detail on the effects of cultural variations on family firm heterogeneity in terms of deviance and dysfunction. Thus far, empirical studies regarding differences in culture and family firm dysfunction are promising. For example, emotional dissonance, i.e., when successors mask their emotions from predecessors, increases conflict in the family and is amplified even further by the family context in Arab cultures, due to religious norms, respect for elders, and paternal authority (Yezza et al., 2021). Wated and Sanchez (2015) found that culturally appropriate human resource practices are needed to curb managerial tolerance of nepotism, which remains an important element of Latin American business culture. Meanwhile, workers in Chinese family firms were found to be more likely to engage in counterproductive work behavior because they perceive low levels of organizational justice, psychological contract violations, and lack of trust due to a Machiavellian work culture operating in the firm (Zheng et al., 2017). Other studies that brought national culture into play mainly examined firms in one country (e.g.,Eddleston & Mulki, 2021; Ghafoor et al., 2019a, 2019b; Jeong et al., 2022) rather than making comparisons across cultures.

Theorists are moving toward cross-cultural comparisons, which indicates that empiricists cannot be far behind. As mentioned in a previous chapter, one theoretical article that applied family science theories to family development explored how Aristotelian versus Confucian traditions shape family firm attitudes and practices (Sison et al., 2020). The authors explained why some attitudes and practices typically seen as dysfunctional and deviant according to Aristotelian culture, such as nepotism, bribery, gift-giving, and guanxi, are not similarly viewed that way through a Confucian lens. Another conceptual article (Samara et al., 2021) proposed that family firms in collectivist cultures are more likely to engage in bifurcation bias regarding compensation that favors family members, due to a strong desire and moral obligation to cater to the family's financial wellbeing, than family firms operating in individualist cultures.

Introducing the potential role that religion may play is an important development in terms of moderating some of the negative behaviors that have dominated this book. Family business leaders' religious beliefs often influence a firm's values and culture through generations (Sorenson, 2013). Recently, Carradus and colleagues (2020) found that when family firm leaders held faith-based values they were more likely to emphasize honesty, trust, and stewardship within their family business. Bringing in the Muslim faith, Alrubaishi et al. (2021) pointed out a lack of research attention to the imprints that Islamic culture, its ethical concepts, and its informal practices have on family businesses in general and in the behavior of Muslim family firms in particular.

Alrubaishi and colleagues proposed that the concept of imprinting is active in transferring these cultural concepts and informal practices between generations in Muslim family firms. Imprinting is a process in which characteristics that reflect strong aspects of an environment are adopted by a subject and then continue in that subject despite subsequent changes in the environment (Marquis and Tilcsik, 2013). In family firms, imprinting has been used to explain why firms take different approaches to innovation (Erdogan et al., 2020), how entrepreneurial legacy is passed to future generations (Jaskiewicz et al., 2015), and how shared stories inspire innovative practices across generations (Kammerlander et al., 2015; Marques et al., 2022). Imprinting has also been linked to negative behaviors and dysfunctional outcomes in family firms (Kidwell et al., 2018). Although a founding family can stamp its firm with a culture, a vision, and even a conflict management style (Alvarado-Alvarez et al., 2021; Eddleston, 2008), the imprints of dysfunctional families may have negative consequences for family firms such as undeserved entitlement, perceived injustice, damaging altruism, and ultimately dysfunctional behavior. All these proposed avenues for additional research across cultures and religions present the prospect of providing additional knowledge regarding the differential impact of dysfunction across families and firms around the world.

A recent appeal to highlight structural foundations of racial disadvantage for underrepresented minority entrepreneurs (Bruton et al., 2023) indicates that such research should also be taking place in the family firm domain. Among other goals, this research avenue is capable of surfacing additional elements of heterogeneity related to dysfunction as family firms owned by racial and ethnic minorities navigate the broader external environment. Although the minority experience has been researched in family science (e.g., James et al., 2018), it has been less examined in the family firm and entrepreneurship literatures. James and colleagues proposed that the concept of racial and ethnic socialization, i.e., how children attain behaviors, perceptions, values, and attitudes of a particular ethnic group, and see themselves as members of that group, be included in the family systems theory conversation. They suggest this would better explain how socialization impacts the views and actions of members of minority families. In the context of family firm dysfunction, race and ethnicity can be viewed in many ways. Three of these include racial discrimination as a form of internal firm-level dysfunction in a non-minority-owned family firm, racial discrimination as an environmental burden on minority-owned family firms, and minority status as a form of family firm heterogeneity (Kidwell et al., 2023). Incorporating these perspectives into future family business research will perhaps better address the linkages between antecedents and behaviors at the individual and family levels with behaviors at the firm and societal levels of analysis and their diverse impact on family firms.

6.8 Concluding Comments

This chapter provides a review of various theoretical approaches and empirical results that can or have been referenced in the research into the heterogeneity of deviance and dysfunction in family firms. Many of these perspectives such as social exchange, interpersonal conflict, agency, stewardship, and socioemotional wealth have been employed in previous research into family firm dysfunction. Theories stemming from the family system, parental control, family-niche-model of birth order and personality, family communication patterns theory as well as developmental and evolutionary psychology seem fertile ground to aid in explaining why there are differences across family firms in terms of dysfunction and deviance. As noted in the chapter, some of this work is already underway.

Bringing in national culture, religion, and race/ethnicity to explain differences across regions, nations, and demographic factors has also begun and can aid understanding of when and why these phenomena occur and the variance in how they are regarded depending on cultural norms. Future researchers face the challenge of incorporating a redefinition of the family into their work and changing values in terms of what should be classified as negative behaviors.

References

Aldrich, H. E., Brumana, M., Campopiano, G., & Minola, T. (2021). Embedded but not asleep: Entrepreneurship and family business research in the 21st century. *Journal of Family Business Strategy, 12*(1), 1–19.

Alrubaishi, D., McAdam, M., & Harrison, R. (2021). Culture, convention, and continuity: Islam and family firm ethical behavior. *Business Ethics, the Environment & Responsibility, 30*(2), 202–215.

Alvarado-Alvarez, C., Armadans, I., Parada, M. J., & Anguera, M. T. (2021). Unraveling the role of shared vision and trust in constructive conflict management of family firms. An empirical study from a mixed methods approach. *Frontiers in Psychology, 12*, 629730.

Bamaca-Colbert, M. Y., Henry, C. S., Perez-Brena, N., Gayles, J. G., & Martinez, G. (2019). Cultural orientation gaps within a family systems perspective. *Journal of Family Theory and Review, 11*(4), 524–543.

Barrena Martínez, J., López Fernández, M., & Romero Fernández, P. M. (2016). Corporate social responsibility: Evolution through institutional and stakeholder perspectives. *European Journal of Management and Business Economics (EJM&BE), 25*(1), 8–14.

Beck, S. J., Miller, A. N., & Frahm, W. A. (2011). An alternative approach to family communication. *Communication Yearbook, 35*, 93–119.

Berrone, P., Cruz, C., Gomez-Mejia, L., & Larraza-Kintana, M. (2010). Socioemotional wealth and corporate responses to institutional pressures: Do family-controlled firms pollute less? *Administrative Sciences, 55*, 82–113.

Blake, L., Bland, B., & Rouncefield-Swales, A. (2022). Estrangement between siblings in adulthood: A qualitative exploration. *Journal of Family Issues*, https://doi.org/10.1177/0192513X211064876

Blanco-Mazagatos, V., Quevedo-Puente, E., & Delgado-Garcia, J. (2016). How agency conflict between family managers and family owners affects performance in wholly family-owned firms: A generational perspective. *Journal of Family Business Strategy, 7*, 167–177.

Block, J., & Wagner, M. (2014). The effect of family ownership on different dimensions of corporate social responsibility: Evidence from large US firms. *Business Strategy and the Environment, 23*, 475–492.
Bowen, M. (1978). *Family therapy in clinical practice*. Jason Aronson Inc.
Broderick, C. B. (1993). *Understanding family process: Basics of family systems theory*. Sage.
Bruton, G. D., Lewis, A., Cerecedo-Lopez, J. A., & Chapman, K. (2023). A racialized view of entrepreneurship: A review and proposal for future research. *Academy of Management Annals, 17*(2), 492–515.
Carradus, A., Zozimo, R., & Discua Cruz, A. (2020). Exploring a faith-led open systems perspective of stewardship in family businesses. *Journal of Business Ethics, 163*, 701–714.
Collin, S. O. Y., & Ahlberg, J. (2012). Blood in the boardroom: Family relationships influencing the functions of the board. *Journal of Family Business Strategy, 3*(4), 207–219.
Combs, J. G., Shanine, K. K., Burrows, S., Allen, J. S., & Pounds, T. W. (2020). What do we know about business families? Setting the stage for leveraging family science theories. *Family Business Review, 33*(1), 38–63.
Conger, R. D. (1981). The assessment of dysfunctional family systems. *Advances in clinical child psychology*, 199–242.
Constantine, L. L. (1983). Dysfunction and failure in open family systems, I: Application of a unified theory. *Journal of Marriage and the Family*, *45*, 725–738.
Cornelissen, J. P., Haslam, S. A., & Balmer, J. M. (2007). Social identity, organizational identity and corporate identity: Towards an integrated understanding of processes, patternings and products. *British Journal of Management, 18*, S1–S16.
Craig, J. B., & Newbert, S. L. (2020). Reconsidering socioemotional wealth: A Smithian-inspired socio-economic theory of decision-making in the family firm. *Journal of Family Business Strategy, 11*(4), 100353.
Cropanzano, R., Anthony, E. L., Daniels, S. R., & Hall, A. V. (2017). Social exchange theory: A critical review with theoretical remedies. *Academy of Management Annals, 11*(1), 479–516.
Cruz, C., Larraza-Kintana, M., Garces-Galdeano, L., & Berrone, P. (2014). Are family firms really more socially responsible? *Entrepreneurship Theory and Practice, 38*(6), 1295–1316.
Davies, P. T., Parry, L. Q., Bascoe, S. M., Martin, M. J., & Cummings, E. M. (2019). Children's vulnerability to interparental conflict: The protective role of sibling relationship quality. *Child Development, 90*(6), 2118–2134.
Davis, P. S., & Harveston, P. D. (2001). The phenomenon of substantive conflict in the family firm: A cross-generational study. *Journal of Small Business Management, 39*(1), 14–30.

Dorrance Hall, E. (2017). The process of family member marginalization: Turning points experienced by "black sheep." *Personal Relationships, 24*(3), 491–512.
Eddleston, K. A. (2008). The prequel to family firm culture and stewardship: The leadership perspective of the founder. *Entrepreneurship Theory and Practice, 32*(6), 1055–1061.
Eddleston, K. A., & Kidwell, R. E. (2012). Parent–child relationships: Planting the seeds of deviant behavior in the family firm. *Entrepreneurship Theory and Practice, 36*(2), 369–386.
Eddleston, K., & Mulki, J. (2021). Differences in family-owned SMEs' ethical behavior: A mixed gamble perspective of family firm tax evasion. *Entrepreneurship Theory and Practice, 45*(4), 767–791.
Erdogan, I., Rondi, E., & De Massis, A. (2020). Managing the tradition and innovation paradox in family firms: A family imprinting perspective. *Entrepreneurship Theory and Practice, 44*, 20-54.
Ertug, G., Kotha, R., & Hedstrom, P. (2020). Kin ties and the performance of new firms: A structural approach. *Academy of Management Review, 63*(6), 1893–1922.
Erikson, E. H. (1963). *Childhood and society*. W.W. Norton and Company.
Fisak, B., & Grills-Taquechel, A. E. (2007). Parental modeling, reinforcement, and information transfer: Risk factors in the development of child anxiety? *Clinical Child and Family Psychology Review, 10*, 213–231.
Fitzpatrick, M. A., & Ritchie, L. D. (1994). Communication schemata within the family. *Human Communication Research, 20*, 275–301.
Galvin, B. M., Lange, D., & Ashforth, B. E. (2015). Narcissistic organizational identification: Seeing oneself as central to the organization's identity. *Academy of Management Review, 40*(2), 163–181.
Gamboni, C. M., Watters, E. R., & Reed-Fitzke, K. (2021). Gender, religious, and political ideologies among three-generation families: Implications for family conflict. *Family Relations, 70*(5), 1529–1545.
Ghafoor, A., Zainudin, R., & Mahdzan, N. S. (2019a). Corporate fraud and information asymmetry in emerging markets: Case of firms subject to enforcement actions in Malaysia. *Journal of Financial Crime, 26*(1), 95–112.
Ghafoor, A., Zainudin, R., & Mahdzan, N. S. (2019b). Factors eliciting corporate fraud in emerging markets: Case of firms subject to enforcement actions in Malaysia. *Journal of Business Ethics, 160*(2), 587–608.
Gilligan, M., Stocker, C. M., & Jewsbury Conger, K. (2020). Sibling relationships in adulthood: Research findings and new frontiers. *Journal of Family Theory & Review, 12*(3), 305–320.
Gomez-Mejia, L.R., Haynes, K.T., Nunez-Nickel, M., Jacobson, K.J.L., & Moyano-Fuentes, J. (2007). Socioemotional wealth and business risks in

family-controlled firms: Evidence from Spanish olive oil mills. *Administrative Science Quarterly*, *52*, 106–137.

Gordon, G., & Nicholson, N. (2008). *Family wars: Classic conflicts in family business and how to deal with them.* Kogan Page.

Haag, K., & Achtenhagen, L. (2021). The impact of divorce on the family business system in SMEs-patterns of coping strategies, commitment, and ownership regulations. *International Journal of Entrepreneurship and Small Business, 44*(4), 335–358.

Handler, W. C. (1991). Key interpersonal relationships of next-generation family members in family firms. *Journal of Small Business Management, 29*(3), 21.

Hudson, S., González-Gómez, H. V., & Claasen, C. (2019). Legitimacy, particularism and employee commitment and justice. *Journal of Business Ethics, 157*(3), 589–603.

Islas-Moreno, A., Muñoz-Rodríguez, M., Santoyo-Cortés, V. H., Martínez-González, E. G., Aguilar-Gallegos, N., & Morris, W. (2021). The role of conflict in the adoption of governance practices in family businesses. *Journal of Family Business Management, 12*(4), 959–980.

James, A. G., Coard, S. I., Fine, M. A., & Rudy, D. (2018). The central roles of race and racism in reframing family systems theory: A consideration of choice and time. *Journal of Family Theory and Review, 10*, 419–433.

Jaskiewicz, P., Uhlenbruck, K., Balkin, D. B., & Reay, T. (2013). Is nepotism good or bad? Types of nepotism and implications for knowledge management. *Family Business Review, 26*(2), 121–139.

Jaskiewicz, P., Combs, J. G., & Rau, S. B. (2015). Entrepreneurial legacy: Toward a theory of how some family firms nurture transgenerational entrepreneurship. *Journal of Business Venturing, 30*, 29–49.

Jayantilal, S., Jorge, S. F., & Palacios, T. M. B. (2016). Effects of sibling competition on family firm succession: A game theory approach. *Journal of Family Business Strategy, 7*(4), 260–268.

Jensen, A. C., Whiteman, S. D., Fingerman, K. L., & Birditt, K. S. (2013). "Life still isn't fair": Parental differential treatment of young adult siblings. *Journal of Marriage and Family, 75*(2), 438–452.

Jeong, S. H., Kim, H., & Kim, H. (2022). Strategic nepotism in family director appointments: Evidence from family business groups in South Korea. *Academy of Management Journal, 65*(2), 656–682.

Kammerlander, C., Dessi, M., Bird, M., Floris, A., & Murru, A. (2015). The impact of shared stories on family firm innovation: A multi-case study. *Family Business Review, 28*(4), 332–354.

Kellermanns, F. W., & Eddleston, K. A. (2007). A family perspective on when conflict benefits family firm performance. *Journal of Business Research, 60*(10), 1048–1057.

Kellermanns, F. W., & Eddleston, K. A. (2004). Feuding families: When conflict does a family firm good. *Entrepreneurship Theory and Practice, 28*(3), 209–228.

Kidwell, R. E., Cox, K. C., & Kloepfer, K. E. (2019). The diversity of deviance: How it can hurt (and help) families and family firms. *The Palgrave handbook of heterogeneity among family firms*, 643–672.

Kidwell, R. E., Eddleston, K. A., & Kellermanns, F. W. (2018). Learning bad habits across generations: How negative imprints affect human resource management in the family firm. *Human Resource Management Review, 28*(1), 5–17.

Kidwell, R. E., Eddleston, K. A., Kidwell, L. A., Cater, J. J., & Howard, E. (2023). *Dysfunctional behavior in family firms across individuals, families, firms, and environments* (Unpublished working paper).

Kim, J., Fairclough, S., & Dibrell, C. (2017). Attention, action, and greenwash in family-influenced firms? Evidence from polluting industries. *Organization & Environment, 30*(4), 304–323.

Kim, T., & Marler, L. (2020). Are non-blood related "family" members treated differently? Determinants of bifurcation bias among family members in the family firm. *Journal of Family Business Management, 12*(1), 136–151.

Koerner, A. F., & Fitzpatrick, M. A. (2002). Toward a theory of family communication. *Communication Theory, 12*(1), 70–91.

Koerner, A. F., Schrodt, P., & Fitzpatrick, M. A. (2017). Family communication patterns theory: A grand theory of family communication. *Engaging theories in family communication*, pp. 142–153.

Kubíček, A., & Machek, O. (2020). Intrafamily conflicts in family businesses: A systematic review of the literature and agenda for future research. *Family Business Review, 33*(2), 194–227.

Kushins, E. R., & Behounek, E. (2020). Using sociological theory to problematize family business research. *Journal of Family Business Strategy, 11*(1), 1–9.

Laursen, B., & Pursell, G. (2009). Conflict in peer relationships. In K. H. Rubin, W. M. Bukowski, & B. Laursen (Eds.), *Handbook of peer interactions, relationships, and groups* (pp. 267–286). The Guilford Press.

Laursen, B., & Veenstra, R. (2021). Toward understanding the functions of peer influence: A summary and synthesis of recent empirical research. *Journal of Research on Adolescence, 31*(4), 889–907.

Levinson, D. J. (1978). *The seasons of a man's life*. Ballantine.

Loeser, M. K., Whiteman, S. D., & McHale, S. M. (2016). Siblings' perceptions of differential treatment, fairness, and jealousy and adolescent adjustment: A moderated indirect effects model. *Journal of Child and Family Studies, 25*, 2405–2414.

Mackey, J. D., McAllister, C. P., Ellen, B. P., III., & Carson, J. E. (2021). A meta-analysis of interpersonal and organizational workplace deviance research. *Journal of Management, 47*, 597–622.

Madison, K., Eddleston, K. A., Kellermanns, F. W., & Powell, G. N. (2021). Kinship and gender in family firms: New insights into employees' organizational citizenship behavior. *Family Business Review, 34*, 270–295.

Maree, J. G. (2021). The psychosocial development theory of Erik Erikson: Critical overview. *Early Child Development and Care, 191*(7–8), 1107–1121.

Marques, P., Bikfalvi, A., & Busquet, F. (2022). A family imprinting approach to nurturing willing successors: Evidence From centennial family firms. *Family Business Review, 35*(3), 246–274.

Marquis, C., & Tilcsik, A. (2013). Imprinting: Toward a multilevel theory. *Academy of Management Annals, 7*, 195–245.

Menesini, E., Camodeca, M., & Nocentini, A. (2010). Bullying among siblings: The role of personality and relational variables. *British Journal of Developmental Psychology, 28*(4), 921–939.

Milevsky, A. (2019). Parental factors, psychological well-being, and sibling dynamics: A mediational model in emerging adulthood. *Marriage & Family Review, 55*(5), 476–492.

Miller, D., & Le Breton-Miller, I. (2014). Deconstructing socioemotional wealth. *Entrepreneurship Theory and Practice, 38*(4), 713–720.

Miller, D., & Le Breton-Miller, I. (2021). Family firms: A breed of extremes? *Entrepreneurship Theory and Practice, 45*(4), 663–681.

Müller, M., Halová, D., Jedličková, L., & Cserge, T. (2022). Existential disruptions of managers as a collapse of childhood patterns: An interpretative phenomenological investigation. *Integrative Psychological and Behavioral Science, 56*, 779–800.

Newbert, S., & Craig, J. B. (2017). Moving beyond socioemotional wealth: Toward a normative theory of decision making in family business. *Family Business Review, 30*(4), 339–346.

Nicholson, N. (2008). Evolutionary psychology and family business: A new synthesis for theory, research, and practice. *Family Business Review, 21*(1), 103–118.

O'Brien, K. E., Minjock, R. M., Colarelli, S. M., & Yang, C. (2018). Kinship ties and employee theft perceptions in family-owned businesses. *European Management Journal, 36*(3), 421–430.

Olson, D. H. (2000). Circumplex model of marital and family systems. *Journal of Family Therapy, 22*(2), 144–167.

Paskewitz, E. A., & Beck, S. J. (2017). When work and family merge: Understanding intragroup conflict experiences in family farm businesses. *Journal of Family Communication, 17*(4), 386–400.

Paulhus, D. L., Trapnell, P. D., & Chen, D. (1999). Birth order effects on personality and achievement within families. *Psychological Science, 10*, 482–488.

Paulhus, D. L., & Williams, K. M. (2002). The Dark Triad of personality: Narcissism, Machiavellianism, and psychopathy. *Journal of Research in Personality, 36*, 556–563.

Purkayastha, S., Veliyath, R., & George, R. (2019). The roles of family ownership and family management in the governance of agency conflicts. *Journal of Business Research, 98*, 50–64.

Qiu, H., & Freel, M. (2020). Managing family-related conflicts in family businesses: A review and research agenda. *Family Business Review, 33*(1), 90–113.

Ritchie, L. D., & Fitzpatrick, M. A. (1990). Family communication patterns measuring intrapersonal perceptions of interpersonal relationships. *Communication Research, 17*, 523–544.

Rodkin, P. C., Espelage, D. L., & Hanish, L. D. (2015). A relational framework for understanding bullying: Developmental antecedents and outcomes. *American Psychologist, 70*(4), 311.

Rosecká, N., & Machek, O. (2022). Non-family members and conflict processes in family firms: A systematic review of literature. *Journal of Business Economics, 92*(2), 235–281.

Samara, G., Jamali, D. & Parada, M. (2021). Antecedents and outcomes of bifurcated compensation in family firms: A multilevel view. *Human Resource Management Review, 31*(1), https://doi.org/10.1016/j.hrmr.2019.100728.

Scharp, K. M. (2019). "You're not welcome here": A grounded theory of family distancing. *Communication Research, 46*(4), 427–455.

Scharp, K. M., & Dorrance Hall, E. (2017). Family marginalization, alienation, and estrangement: Questioning the nonvoluntary status of family relationships. *Annals of the International Communication Association, 41*(1), 28–45.

Scharp, K. M., Thomas, L. J., & Paxman, C. G. (2015). "It was the straw that broke the camel's back": Exploring the distancing processes communicatively constructed in parent-child estrangement backstories. *Journal of Family Communication, 15*(4), 330–348.

Schulze, W., Lubatkin, M., Dino, R., & Buchholtz, A. (2001). Agency relationships in family firms: Theory and evidence. *Organization Science, 12*(2), 99–116.

Shanine, K. K., Madison, K., Combs, J. G., & Eddleston, K. A. (2023). Parenting the successor: It starts at home and leaves an enduring impact on the family business. *Entrepreneurship Theory and Practice, 47*(4), 1093–1131.

Simons, R. L., Whitbeck, L. B., Conger, R. D., & Wu, C.-I. (1991). Intergenerational transmission of harsh parenting. *Developmental Psychology, 27*(1), 159–171.

Sison, A., Ferrero, I., & Redin, D. (2020). Some virtue ethics implications from Aristotelian and Confucian perspectives on family and business. *Journal of Business Ethics, 165*, 241–254.

Soleimanof, S., Morris, M. H., & Jang, Y. (2021). Following the footsteps that inspire: Parental passion, family communication, and children's entrepreneurial attitudes. *Journal of Business Research, 128*, 450–461.

Sorenson, R. L. (2013). How moral and social values become embedded in family firms. *Journal of Management, Spirituality & Religion, 10*(2), 116–137.

Spranger, J. L., Colarelli, S. M., Dimotakis, N., Jacob, A. C., & Arvey, R. D. (2012). Effects of kin density within family-owned businesses. *Organizational Behavior and Human Decision Processes, 119*(2), 151–162.

Stewart, A. (2020). (2020) Family control, ambivalence, and preferential benefits. *Journal of Family Business Strategy, 11*(4), 100352. https://doi.org/10.1016/j.jfbs.2020.100352

Sulloway, F. J. (1996). *Born to rebel: Birth order, family dynamics, and creative lives*. Pantheon Books.

Wated, G., & Sanchez, J. I. (2015). Managerial tolerance of nepotism: The effects of individualism–collectivism in a Latin American context. *Journal of Business Ethics, 130*(1), 45–57.

Waterwall, B. & Alipour, K. (2021). Nonfamily employees' perceptions of treatment in family businesses: Implications for organizational attraction, job pursuit intentions, work attitudes, and turnover intentions. *Journal of Family Business Strategy, 12*(3), https://doi.org/10.1016/j.jfbs.2020.100387.

Yezza, H., Chabaud, D., & Calabrò, A. (2021). Conflict dynamics and emotional dissonance during the family business succession process: Evidence from the Tunisian context. *Entrepreneurship Research Journal, 11*(3), 219–244.

Yoho, M., Faur, S., & Laursen, B. (2022). Conflict moderates the longitudinal association between aggression with classmates and popularity: Leveraging disagreements into peer status. *Personality and Individual Differences, 190*, 111538.

Xiang, D., Worthington, A., & Higgs, H. (2014). Family ownership, altruism, and agency costs in Australian small- and medium-sized enterprises. *Applied Economics, 46*(32), 3907–3921.

Yu, X., Stanley, L., Li, Y., Eddleston, K., & Kellermanns, F. W. (2020). The invisible hand of evolutionary psychology: The importance of kinship in first generation family firms. *Entrepreneurship Theory and Practice, 44*(1), 134–157.

Zachary, R. K., Danes, S. M., & Balabram, E. (2023). *Concise introduction to the family firm (part of the Elgar Concise Introduction Series).* Edward Elgar Publishing Limited.

Zheng, W., Wu, Y. C. J., Chen, X., & Lin, S. J. (2017). Why do employees have counterproductive work behavior? The role of founder's Machiavellianism and the corporate culture in China. *Management Decision, 55*(3), 563–578.

CHAPTER 7

Diversity of Deviance and Dysfunction: Implications for Future Study

Abstract Implications for future theoretical and empirical work in the heterogeneity of dysfunction and deviance in family firms are discussed. Research that considers various types of potentially deviant or dysfunctional behavior in family firms is integrated, resulting in a proposed multi-level framework that potentially cuts across individuals, families, firms, and environments. Such a model can help organize research in this diverse area of scholarly and practical concern that transcends academic disciplines. The concept of microfoundations is used to link behavior by individuals and small groups to effects at the family, firm, and environmental levels. Alternative views of motivation to commit dysfunctional behavior are presented. Anecdotes from real-life examples are used throughout to highlight the connection between academic research and practical application.

Keywords Socioecological model of family firm dysfunction · Microfoundations theory · Fraud triangle · Cross-disciplinary research · Pressure · Opportunity · Rationalization · Organizational culture change

R. E. Kidwell, *Dysfunction and Deviance Across Family Firms*, Palgrave Studies in Family Business Heterogeneity,
https://doi.org/10.1007/978-3-031-51816-4_7

Kevin and Delroy grew up together as cousins in Jamaica. As a teen, Delroy went to live with his aunt in New York City. Not long after his arrival, Delroy became involved in criminal activities such as theft and drug dealing but managed to avoid jail despite some criminal charges. A few years later, Kevin arrived in Atlanta to attend college. The pair reconnected there as Delroy thought it would give him a fresh start.

A few years later, Kevin went on to medical school in New Orleans, and once again Delroy followed him not long after. They became roommates despite Delroy's seeming inability to stay out of trouble. A few years later, Kevin, now married and starting a family, opened his medical practice in Louisiana. He soon hired Delroy as a billing specialist, and eventually Delroy became office manager. Most of the practitioners in Kevin's specialty employed family members because relatives were thought to be trusted to have the doctor's best interest at heart. While motivated by this industry norm, Kevin was more driven by the prospect of providing his cousin with an opportunity to make an honest living. The hire and rise of Delroy to manager came despite concerns of Kevin's immediate family, some of whom were also employed at the practice.

Delroy appeared to thrive in his position and eventually contacted other local medical practitioners hoping to create more business for himself as a biller for them as well. However, those practitioners were skeptical. As Delroy was seen driving luxury vehicles and making other big-ticket purchases, Kevin's colleagues and family began to whisper that given Delroy's past, Kevin should pay more attention to his office finances as Delroy might be stealing from him. Kevin often met these concerns with assertions that his cousin was simply well-paid and appreciated, and that their worries were due to Delroy's past. The whispers got louder but Kevin continued to defiantly ignore the chatter until he could no longer.

One day, Kevin received notice that he was being investigated for suspicion of defrauding the state's Medicaid program. Given that all billing was filed using Kevin's medical license number, he was responsible for the fraud that occurred in his office even though Delroy was the one committing the crimes, and Kevin had no knowledge of it. Investigators found that one type of procedure being billed by Kevin's practice was over twice that of all the other local practitioners within his specialty combined. Kevin was shocked, then angry, and then confused. He was shocked that all this could happen under his nose, and angry that Delroy engaged in fraud from the state government and even stole from Kevin himself. The young doctor now faced the loss of his practice, fines, and jail time because he was responsible for the fraud. And finally, he was confused because he thought of his cousin as family.

Kevin hired and later promoted Delroy because he was family. Kevin trusted Delroy because he was family. Kevin ignored the whispers about theft because Delroy was family. Ultimately, Kevin lost his medical practice, had to repay the state for Delroy's fraud, and had to relocate with his family to another state because of his cousin's crimes. Fortunately, Kevin avoided criminal charges; Delroy went to prison. The state and its taxpayers lost millions.

The anecdote, based on a true story related by one of Kevin's family members to the author, illustrates several elements of heterogeneity in the causes, acts, and effects of deviance and dysfunction in the family firm. Hiring one family member, a cousin perhaps with a Machiavellian capability to manipulate and control the family leader, led to the destruction of the family business through theft from within and fraud committed against the state. Many other family firms hire family members effectively and are never faced with these concerns. The state was severely affected by the fraud while the family firm leader lost his business and other employees lost their jobs due to the theft and fraud committed by Delroy. Fraud perpetrated against the government by family firms is relatively unusual, yet it happened in this case because the family firm leader did not listen to others who suspected something was amiss. The trusting family firm leader was manipulated by the trusted family member. Obviously, it happens—but rarely, and not typically when there is vigilant family firm leadership.

The case of Kevin and Delroy involves individual-level antecedents (the Dark Triad trait of Machiavellianism and the firm and family context of altruistic behavior on the part of the leader toward a family member). It describes an inwardly directed dysfunctional behavior (theft) resulting from the trait and the context that damages another family member, his family, and his firm (the doctor's practice went under and the family had to move to another state). It includes an outwardly directed dysfunctional behavior (fraud) that damages external stakeholders (taxpayers who finance the state Medicaid system). In this single example, one individual committing deviant and dysfunctional acts affects other individuals, the family, the family firm, and ultimately society in various ways. Many elements in this short story illustrate the heterogeneity of deviant and dysfunctional behavior (cause, act, outcome) in a way that is unique to family firms—but not all family firms.

7.1 Family Firm Heterogeneity and Dysfunction

Family firm researchers have examined the complexity of heterogeneity of family business by considering categories, configurations, and types of family firms (Daspit et al., 2021) in terms of family firm governance (Nordqvist et al., 2014), differing values that result in unique family firm designs (Rau et al., 2019), and variance of family involvement that result in different ways to classify family businesses (Shanker & Astrachan, 1996; Sharma, 2002).

More relevant to this book is a consideration of the variability of conditions to be found in family firms. This emphasis relates to past investigations regarding variance in technological innovation (De Massis et al., 2013), in performance (Su et al., 2019), in R&D investment (Chrisman & Patel, 2012), and in social capital (Herrero, 2018)—and in providing a rationale for these variations across family businesses. Researchers also find variation in conditions regarding deviance and dysfunction in family firms. These include variability in what types of antecedents lead to deviant and dysfunctional behaviors; differences in the types of negative acts themselves, their perpetrators, and their motives; diversity in who is targeted by these behaviors as well as differences in their impact on the individual, family, family firm, and the external environment.

The research recounted in this book and the true stories provided along with it reveal that the prevalence and nature of deviant and dysfunctional behavior will vary across family firms based on individual personalities, individual perceptions, firm context, family and early childhood influences, types of families, organizational as well as national cultures, and other conditions in the surrounding environment. Similar variation can be observed regarding the impact of these acts. In some instances, the negative effects are devastating to the different targets and in other instances can be positive or even strategic to all or some of those involved as perpetrators and even targets. Thus, all these variations across family firms *depend* on the circumstances—and the previous chapters have provided clues on how, why, and when we can expect conditions to be ripe for those negative acts to occur.

The rest of this chapter provides ideas on how differences across family firms might be examined in future research by introducing a socioecological model in which to view deviance and dysfunction in family firms, by discussing how individual dysfunction in the family firm connects with dysfunction at other levels of analysis using the microfoundations concept, and by proposing motivations that drive individuals—in their roles as family members, employees, managers, and leaders—to engage in negative behaviors that define dysfunction and often deviance as well.

7.2 Framing Future Research: A Socioecological Approach

Studies of dysfunction in family firms juxtapose individuals within the dominant family, the family firm, and the environment; the dominant family within the family firm and the environment; and the interactions of the firm with the external environment. Although a great deal of family firm dysfunction research compares family firms to non-family firms on issues such as tax avoidance, fraud, gender discrimination and others, there has been a strong movement in recent years toward studying dysfunction across family firms and not just making comparisons about general types.

A better understanding of the heterogeneity of family firms that can guide future research into dysfunctional behavior may be gained by considering the phenomena within a multi-level socioecological model. Such models were first advanced as a context to the study of raising children (Bronfenbrenner, 1979), and they have been more recently applied to such areas as public health (Golden et al., 2015), disparities in occupational exposures to health risks (Ingram et al., 2021), sustainable supply chain management (Dentoni et al., 2021), and generational identity in the workplace (Lyons et al., 2019). This perspective goes beyond interactive models of family systems such as circumplex theory (Olson, 2000) as applied to family firms (e.g., Daspit et al., 2018), and the three-circle model of the family business system (Tagiuri & Davis, 1996) to encourage research across levels of analysis.

A socioecological model of family firm dysfunction encourages future researchers to think about multiple levels of analysis to better understand the drivers, processes, and outcomes of dysfunction, as well as an effective means to understand the complexity of how individual dysfunctional behavior in family firms is shaped by the intersection of influences at the individual, family, firm, and societal levels (Lyons et al., 2019; Ingram et al., 2021). The model implies that research should cut across levels of analysis thus providing the need for multi-level theories that imply further study encompassing not only the individual and the family but the firm and its external environment. As emphasized by the research reviewed in the previous chapters, these levels generally impact each other in different ways in varying circumstances across family firms. A socioecological perspective nests the individual in not only the family firm, but the family system itself, as well as the external environment, with all levels potentially interacting with one another as seen in Fig. 7.1 to potentially impact behavior of all types.

Working in from the top edge of the figure, the environmental influences on firm, family, and individual include those discussed in Chapter 2

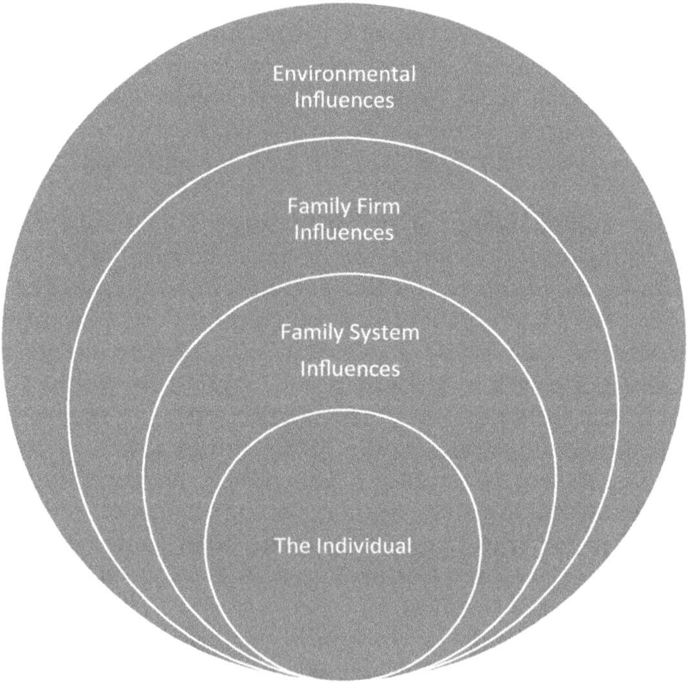

Fig. 7.1 Socioecological influences on individual dysfunctional behavior in family firms

(weak institutions and weak legal protections) and Chapter 6 (cross-cultural differences in defining dysfunction and deviance). The family firm influences were discussed in Chapter 2 (entitlement, altruism, nepotism practices, pursuit of socioemotional wealth) while the family system influences were discussed in both Chapter 2 (early child interactions, parenting style) and Chapter 6 (the nature and the impact of the family system on the individual). Meanwhile, an individual, whose mindset is shaped by these influences, brings personality, attitude, status, and other factors, which also influence behavior, in this instance the likelihood of involvement in negative acts.

A business family's pursuit of socioemotional wealth and that pursuit's implications for dysfunctional behavior inside and outside the family firm exemplify the usefulness of the socioecological model in that SEW (unique to family firms) crosses levels of analysis to explain relationships—functional and dysfunctional—among individuals, families, family firms, and external stakeholders. SEW is acted upon by individuals, is inspired by the family's and family firm's values and desires, is realized at the family and firm levels, and often involves members of the firm reaching into the external environment in pursuit of its goals. At the individual level, SEW has been seen to lessen the effects of dysfunctional work behavior in some instances (McLarty & Holt, 2019) and at the firm level to motivate leaders to pursue non-economic goals such as identity, influence, and continuity for the family firm (Gomez-Mejia et al., 2007; Swab et al., 2020). Yet, it has also inspired behaviors that damage those inside and outside the family and the firm (Zientara, 2017). Several studies have used SEW as a perspective when considering bifurcation bias (e.g., Samara et al., 2021), corporate social irresponsibility (e.g., Cabeza-Garcia et al., 2017), and interpersonal conflict (Rousseau et al., 2018). Thus, SEW is a key concept when considering differences in dysfunction across family firms and levels of analysis.

7.3 Microfoundations of Dysfunctional Behavior in Family Firms

Adding to the discussion of cross level analysis is the concept of microfoundations, which tries to grasp how individual actions relate and connect to firm-level or even societal-level results (Felin et al., 2015). The application of microfoundations to family firm research helps in understanding the interconnectedness of an individual's behavior to the family and to the family firm (De Massis & Foss, 2018). Table 7.1 places antecedents, behaviors, and outcomes of deviant and dysfunctional behavior, which were discussed in more detail in previous chapters, grouped by levels of analysis to indicate how one person's behavior potentially impacts the family, the family firm, and the external environment. The table implies potential connections between behavior at the micro level and outcomes at the family, firm, and societal levels, and vice versa. Future study of differences across firms in terms of negative behaviors may be aided by a microfoundations application.

Table 7.1 Multi-level view of dysfunctional behavior in family firms

Individual level	*Family level*	*Firm level*	*Environment level*
Antecedents	**Antecedents**	**Antecedents**	**Antecedents**
Early Interactions	Role Making	IP Conflict	Weak institutions
Role Taking	Parenting Style	Nepotism	Weak legal protection
Personality	Birth Order	Pursuit of SEW	Pervasive corruption
Affect/Emotion	Communication	Governance	Cultural differences
IP Conflict	IP Conflict	Firm Performance	Definition of family
Behaviors	**Behaviors**	**Behaviors directed inside**	**Behaviors directed outside**
Shirking	Bullying	Bifurcation bias	Fraud
Bullying	Abuse	Sex discrimination	Financial Misconduct
Theft	Sibling rivalry	Firm conflict	Bribery
Insubordination	Family conflict		Tax avoidance
Resisting Change			Tax evasion
Substance abuse			CSIR
Outcomes	**Outcomes**	**Outcomes**	**Outcomes**
Victimization	Family Dysfunction	Performance	Loss of tax revenue
Punishment	Family Relations	Financial Gain	Financial losses
Monetary gain	Alienation	Succession	Customer losses
Emotional gain	Marginalization	Governance	Environmental damage
Job Loss	Estrangement	Reputation	More corruption
Alienation	Divorce		
Marginalization	Family factions		
Estrangement			

The opening vignette to this chapter demonstrates the impact of individual behavior (theft and fraud) on the firm and on the larger society. Delroy's theft of funds from Kevin and his fraud on the Medicaid system had huge ramifications for the medical practice (destroyed) and the government (loss of millions in taxpayer dollars that went illegally to Delroy). Family relationships were also damaged, if not ended, due to one person's behavior. Similar connections to macro-level impact analysis can be seen in several cases already discussed in which individuals stole funds, committed fraud, bribed local officials, or otherwise engaged in negative actions that hurt others. John Rigas, Bernie Madoff, and François-Henri Pinault exemplify family firm leaders whose individual behavior had negative effects on their family firm's survival or reputation, and on external stakeholders. Individual leaders who establish policies that lead to unlawful discrimination, social irresponsibility, and tax avoidance create situations resulting in negative outcomes in the external environment.

Conversely, phenomena in the macroenvironment can also impact individual behavior. Conditions such as weak institutions, poor legal protections, cultural differences, and an atmosphere of pervasive corruption can lead individuals to take actions that may be damaging to themselves, their families, and their family firms. A business environment where bribery or facilitation payments are standard affects the behavior of individual participants who may see no way to carry on the family firm without engaging in illegal or unethical acts.

Finally, the impact of the family, operating inside or outside the business, is important to consider. The family members' actions (parents, siblings, children, and more distant kin) affect the individual behavior of family members, in some cases leading to a dysfunctional family and eventual estrangement of individuals from other members of the family. The family members who initiate such actions may not even be engaged in the business, but they can do things that affect family firm members, leaders, and the firm itself such as placing their children into scapegoat or hero roles, bullying and abusing other family members, and triggering interpersonal conflict.

7.4 Motivational Differences Across Family Firms

Obviously, different family firms have variations in personalities, contexts, family relationships, external environmental conditions, and other factors that would serve as antecedents to the occurrence of dysfunctional behavior. As noted in Chapter 2, there are also disparities in the workings of the social exchange process and the application of violations of the psychological contract that need to be accounted for across family firms. These variables would seem to act as both antecedents and moderators when examining their relationship to the occurrence of dysfunctional behaviors directed inside as well as outside the firm. Another motivator that might indicate the occurrence of dysfunction can be found in the accounting literature.

The fraud triangle (Cressey, 1953) was first proposed in the study of white-collar crime to help explain why individuals commit fraud in their organizations. Interviews with those imprisoned for fraud produced three factors that seemed key in motivating these individuals to engage in dysfunctional behavior. First, there was personal pressure such as debt or an incentive such as bonuses tied to financial metrics that factored in the perpetrators' commission of fraud (Ramos, 2003). Second, there was an opportunity to engage in fraud including weak internal control systems, a culture of dishonesty, inability of management to judge the quality of performance, or failure to discipline fraud perpetrators (Albrecht et al., 2006). Finally, perpetrators who committed fraud could rationalize their actions by claiming unfair treatment, perceiving that everyone else is committing fraud, and/or not regarding stealing as wrong. Ramos (2003: 28) explained such rationalization this way: "Those involved in a fraud are able to rationalize a fraudulent act as being consistent with their personal code of ethics. Some individuals possess an attitude, character, or set of ethical values that allows them to knowingly and intentionally commit a dishonest act."

Whereas a few researchers have framed studies of family business fraud with the fraud triangle (e.g., Ghafoor et al., 2019), the idea that various forms of pressure, opportunity, and rationalization serve as motivators to commit other dysfunctional acts deserves more thought. The fraud triangle model might be applied to family firms in a way that goes beyond financial dysfunction and links relationships between the individuals, the family, and the firm regarding other forms of dysfunction. Such an application may assist in examining the microfoundations of dysfunctional behavior whose effects are felt across levels of analysis. For example, Jane, a family member, may perceive she is being pressured by a relative to hire an unqualified cousin who would hurt the firm. The family member has the opportunity to make the hire due to her position as HR manager and can rationalize her decision because hiring the cousin will avoid conflict with other members of the family, and conflict avoidance is a big part of the family culture.

As Schuchter and Levi (2016) stress, all of the fraud triangle elements are highly influenced by the corporate culture in the companies of the perpetrators. In the same way, pressure, opportunity, and rationalization to engage in dysfunctional behavior can be guided by family values and firm culture in a wide range of dysfunctional behaviors, providing another clue as to why bad behavior varies across family firms. Virtuous and dubious values become part of a culture that is perpetuated by storytelling and likely will stay part of the culture until a new leader arrives with different stories that attempt to break the cycle and establish a culture change (Barney et al., 2023). For example, the authoritarian/paternalistic culture of one family firm where the author was employed continued long after the company was purchased by an outside corporation. The dysfunctional culture was preserved by decades-old stories of a tyrannical manager who inspired employees to escape his wrath by hiding from him in a closet and of the family giving an annual Christmas ham to the nonfamily employees. These stories sent mixed signals as to what values the family was attempting to promote. Eventually, new stories emphasizing new values were needed to transform the culture into a more professional organization.

7.5 Concluding Comments

Research into differences in deviant and dysfunctional behavior in families and family firms reaches across many academic disciplines. These disciplines represent scholarly work in such fields as family business; strategy; ethics; entrepreneurship; human resource management; organizational, social, evolutionary, and developmental psychology; family science; family therapy; communications; accounting; finance; and economics. The fact that so many researchers are interested in these topics yet not many have crossed into other subject areas indicates that additional multidisciplinary research is desirable to link more clearly, for example, family therapy with family business, ethics with family science, and communication with human resource management.

Cross-disciplinary inquiry would provide scholars added opportunity to connect different theoretical perspectives that may provide intriguing explanations for the diversity of dysfunction in the family business among individuals, families, and firms. There seem to be rich possibilities in topics that have been largely neglected including the effects of counterproductive behavior at work on dysfunction within the family and on firm-level performance, the relationship of the dysfunctional family to the operations of the family firm, the application of evolutionary psychology to dysfunctional behavior that is directed externally by the firm's leaders, the effects of elements in accounting's fraud triangle in motivating all manner of dysfunctional behavior in family firms as just discussed, and the impact of national cultures and racial socialization on the propensity for individuals, families, and family firms to engage in behavior that has negative consequences for themselves and the environments in which they operate.

In discussing various types of deviance, dysfunction, and "bad" behavior in family firms and seemingly dwelling on the negative in this book, it is important to recall that some deviant behaviors can have constructive results for the individual, the family, the firm, and the external stakeholders. It is also crucial to remember that many family firms do not experience the high levels of negative behavior that are a major focus of this work. This not only illustrates the heterogeneity of family firms, but it is also a testament to the hard work that many family firms and their advisors have put in to figure out a means to deal with conflict and other sources of negative behaviors before they do serious harm. Yet, the horror stories that have been recounted and the research that attempts to identify the causes and effects of negative behavior in family firms are vital to keep in mind as families and their family businesses continue their efforts to provide high-quality products and services that help drive the world's economies.

References

Albrecht, W. S., Albrecht, C. C., & Albrecht, C. O. (2006). *Fraud examination* (2nd ed.). Thomson South-Western.

Barney, J., Amorim, M., & Júlio, C. (2023). *The secret of culture change*. Berrett-Koehler.

Bronfenbrenner, U. (1979). *The ecology of human development: Experiments by nature and design*. Harvard University Press.

Cabeza-Garcia, L., Sacristan-Navarro, M., & Gomez-Anson, S. (2017). Family involvement and corporate social responsibility disclosure. *Journal of Family Business Strategy, 9*, 109–122.

Chrisman, J. J., & Patel, P. C. (2012). Variations in R&D investments of family and nonfamily firms: Behavioral agency and myopic loss aversion perspectives. *Academy of Management Journal, 55*(4), 976–997.

Cressey, D. R. (1953). *Other people's money*. The Free Press.

Daspit, J. J., Chrisman, J. J., Ashton, T., & Evangelopoulos, N. (2021). Family firm heterogeneity: A definition, common themes, scholarly progress, and directions forward. *Family Business Review, 34*(3), 296–322.

Daspit, J. J., Madison, K., Barnett, T., & Long, R. G. (2018). The emergence of bifurcation bias from unbalanced families: Examining HR practices in the family firm using circumplex theory. *Human Resource Management Review, 28*(1), 18–32.

De Massis, A., Frattini, F., & Lichtenthaler, U. (2013). Research on technological innovation in family firms: Present debates and future directions. *Family Business Review, 26*(1), 10–31.

De Massis, A., & Foss, N. J. (2018). Advancing family business research: The promise of microfoundations. *Family Business Review, 31*(4), 386–396.

Dentoni, D., Pinkse, J., & Lubberink, R. (2021). Linking sustainable business models to socio-ecological resilience through cross-sector partnerships: A complex adaptive systems view. *Business & Society, 60*(5), 1216–1252.

Felin, T., Foss, N. J., & Ployhart, R. E. (2015). The microfoundations movement in strategy and organization theory. *Academy of Management Annals, 9*(1), 575–632.

Ghafoor, A., Zainudin, R., & Mahdzan, N. S. (2019). Corporate fraud and information asymmetry in emerging markets: Case of firms subject to enforcement actions in Malaysia. *Journal of Financial Crime, 26*(1), 95–112.

Golden, S.D., McLeroy, K.R., Green, L.W., Earp, J.A.L. & Lieberman, L.D. (2015). Upending the social ecological model to guide health promotion efforts toward policy and environmental change. *Health Education & Behavior*, *42*(1_suppl), 8S-14S

Gomez-Mejia, L. R., Haynes, K. T., Nunez-Nickel, M., Jacobson, K. J. L., & Moyano-Fuentes, J. (2007). Socioemotional wealth and business risks in family-controlled firms: Evidence from Spanish olive oil mills. *Administrative Science Quarterly, 52*, 106–137.

Herrero, I. (2018). How familial is family social capital? Analyzing bonding social capital in family and nonfamily firms. *Family Business Review, 31*(4), 441–459.

Ingram, M., Wolf, A. M. A., López-Gálvez, N. I., Griffin, S. C., & Beamer, P. I. (2021). Proposing a social ecological approach to address disparities in occupational exposures and health for low-wage and minority workers employed in small businesses. *Journal of Exposure Science & Environmental Epidemiology, 31*(3), 404–411.

Lyons, S. T., Schweitzer, L., Urick, M. J., & Kuron, L. (2019). A dynamic social-ecological model of generational identity in the workplace. *Journal of Intergenerational Relationships, 17*(1), 1–24.

McLarty, B. D., & Holt, D. T. (2019). A bright side to family firms: How socioemotional wealth importance affects dark traits–job performance relationships. *Family Business Review, 32*(4), 378–395.

Nordqvist, M., Sharma, P., & Chirico, F. (2014). Family firm heterogeneity and governance: A configuration approach. *Journal of Small Business Management, 52*(2), 192–209.

Olson, D. H. (2000). Circumplex model of marital and family systems. *Journal of Family Therapy, 22*(2), 144–167.

Ramos, M. (2003, January). Auditors' responsibility for fraud detection. *Journal of Accountancy, 195*(1), 28–36.

Rau, S. B., Schneider-Siebke, & Gunther, C. (2019). Family firm values explaining family firm heterogeneity. *Family Business Review, 32*(2), 195–215.

Rousseau, M. B., Kellermanns, F., Zellweger, T., & Beck, T. E. (2018). Relationship conflict, family name congruence, and socioemotional wealth in family firms. *Family Business Review, 31*(4), 397–416.

Samara, G., Jamali, D., & Parada, M. (2021). Antecedents and outcomes of bifurcated compensation in family firms: A multilevel view. *Human Resource Management Review, 31*(1), https://doi.org/10.1016/j.hrmr.2019.100728.

Schuchter, A., & Levi, M. (2016). The fraud triangle revisited. *Security Journal, 29*, 107–121.

Sharma, P. (2002, August). Stakeholder mapping technique: Toward the development of a family firm typology. In *62nd meeting of the Academy of Management, Denver, August* (pp. 1–25).

Shanker, M. C., & Astrachan, J. H. (1996). Myths and realities: Family businesses' contribution to the US economy—A framework for assessing family business statistics. *Family Business Review, 9*(2), 107–123.

Su, E., Holt, D. T., & Pollack, J. M. (2019). The distribution of family firm performance heterogeneity: Understanding power law distributions. *The Palgrave handbook of heterogeneity among family firms* (pp. 407–429).

Swab, R. G., Sherlock, C., Markin, E., & Dibrell, C. (2020). "SEW" What do we know and where do we go? A review of socioemotional wealth and a way forward. *Family Business Review, 33*(4), 424–445.

Tagiuri, R., & Davis, J. (1996). Bivalent attributes of the family firm. *Family Business Review, 9*(2), 199–208.

Zientara, P. (2017). Socioemotional wealth and corporate social responsibility: A critical analysis. *Journal of Business Ethics, 144*(1), 185–199.

Index

R. E. Kidwell, *Dysfunction and Deviance Across Family Firms*, Palgrave Studies in Family Business Heterogeneity,
https://doi.org/10.1007/978-3-031-51816-4

GPSR Compliance
The European Union's (EU) General Product Safety Regulation (GPSR) is a set of rules that requires consumer products to be safe and our obligations to ensure this.

If you have any concerns about our products, you can contact us on

ProductSafety@springernature.com

In case Publisher is established outside the EU, the EU authorized representative is:

Springer Nature Customer Service Center GmbH
Europaplatz 3
69115 Heidelberg, Germany

www.ingramcontent.com/pod-product-compliance
Ingram Content Group UK Ltd.
Pitfield, Milton Keynes, MK11 3LW, UK
UKHW021031041026
15470UKWH00014B/1389
9783031518157